LITTLE BOOK OF
FLY FISHING
FOR TROUT

LITTLE BOOK OF
FLY FISHING
FOR TROUT

First published in the UK in 2013

© G2 Entertainment Limited 2013

www.G2ent.co.uk

Printed and bound in Europe

ISBN 978-1-782812-04-3

Contents

4   Introduction

6   The Fish

15   The Food of the Trout

28   Tackle and Methods

35   Care and Conservation

38   Mastering the Cast

46   River Fishing

66   Understanding Lakes

80   An Introduction to Sea Trout Fishing

95   Acknowledgements & Bibliography

Introduction

The sport of fly fishing for trout takes the angler to the most beautiful places these islands have to offer, from the wild, rushing rivers of the north and west to the pellucid streams of the chalk country, lakes, both natural and man-made, and the little tarns and lochs of the hill country. Yet however delightful the scenery and fascinating the wildlife, the urge to outwit a fish or two and have something to show for your trip is not to be denied. In this book the authors, both highly-experienced trout anglers who have fished across the length and breadth of Great Britain, set out the basics for the novice trout angler, providing an introduction to the trout's environment, the food it hunts for, the artificial flies which may be expected to deceive it and the tackle and techniques you will need to present them successfully.

The Fish

The trout is a fascinating fish – in fact, several fascinating fish. In the UK we have the native brown trout (Salmo trutta), which has been swimming the lakes and rivers of Europe on and off since before man began to walk upright, and the rainbow trout (Oncorhynchus mykiss), a much more recent American import. We also have the sea trout, a brown trout which has developed the habit of going to sea to feed. All three have their own distinctive characteristics, and present their own attractions and challenges from the angler's point of view.

The Brown Trout

The brown trout is thought to have evolved as a species around four million years ago, its closest relative being the Atlantic salmon. It has been swimming the rivers and lakes of Europe

Above: *Sea trout*

and some parts of Asia and North Africa ever since, colonising every suitable body of water from tiny streams to estuaries and deep mountain lakes. Fluctuations in the global climate over this time have led to repeated changes in its habitat, which has helped to make it an exceptionally variable and adaptable fish.

The trout has been confusing naturalists for centuries. It comes in so many colour forms and shapes that it seems to be several hundred species rolled into one. For decades these forms were all shoehorned into one species, but the zoologists have recently reclassified it as 28 species. There are some places, such as Lough Melvin in Ireland and Lake Ohrid in Albania, where three or four species of brown trout have evolved in the same lake, each pursuing different food and spawning in different places at different times.

The brown trout is an exceptionally adaptable creature which grows according to the food available to it. In poorly-fed acidic upland lochs and streams, the fish may mature when they are not much more than six inches long and weigh no more than a few ounces, whereas in rich lowland waters they can reach 10lb (4.5kg) or more. In lakes where they have adopted a fish diet, they may grow to twenty or thirty pounds.

The brown trout feeds mainly on a range of small aquatic invertebrates, notably the larvae of various flies, beetles and bugs, often adding small fish to this diet. It is highly opportunistic and will quickly learn to find and catch whatever small creatures are available. It tends to live longer and grow more slowly than the rainbow trout, and is better adapted to low-light conditions – two possible reasons why it has acquired the reputation of being harder to catch than the rainbow.

The Sea Trout

The brown trout has evolved an extraordinary ability – it can switch to a sea-going life, like the Atlantic salmon, in order to take advantage of the richer food supply available in salt water. For many years anglers laboured under the impression that the sea trout was a separate species – it certainly looks different, its bright silver scales making it appear more like a salmon than a trout. In fact we now know that the brown trout and sea trout in a river may actually be each others' parents and children, or brothers and sisters.

In acidic, poorly-fed rivers like many of those of northern and western Britain, the best option for the trout when they are not occupied with spawning is to go to sea to feed, if they can. A seafood diet transforms a trout's prospects, enabling it to grow into a silver torpedo which may reach 10lb, even 20lb in weight.

The few small resident trout that stay in the river may all be males. The male fish do not have the same incentive to go to sea as the females - being big is a great advantage to a female fish, because it enables it to lay more and bigger eggs.

Trout that go to sea will spend most of the winter and spring months roaming the coastal waters near the river of their birth, feeding on sandeels, brit and other small fish, before returning in the spring or summer in preparation for breeding in the late autumn, like the salmon. But unlike salmon, which usually breed only once or twice in their lives, sea trout will return to the spawning redds year after year; one Scottish fish weighing 12½lb was 19 years old and had spawned 11 times.

Though the sea trout belongs to the same species as the brown trout, its behaviour in the river is quite different. Most mature sea trout do not attempt to feed once they have entered the river; in fact they lose all appetite for food. Like the salmon, they concentrate on staying out of trouble and avoiding their many enemies – fish-eating birds, otters, and of course anglers. When they take a fly or lure, they do so out of aggression or curiosity, or possibly force of habit.

The Rainbow Trout

Above: *Rainbow Trout*

The rainbow trout is more closely related to the various Pacific salmon species than it is to the brown trout, its natural home being the western coastal states of the USA. But like the brown, the rainbow has been introduced in suitable areas around the world, both for its sporting merits and its value as a food fish.

The rainbow is readily distinguished from the brown by the pink band along the flank and the many small black spots, which cover the tail and other fins as well as the body; no brown trout ever has spots on its tail. In the water, the rainbow usually has a slightly greenish look when seen from above compared with the brown, which usually looks greyish or brownish. Anatomically however, the two species are very similar, reflecting their similar lifestyles and diet.

Brown trout and rainbows essentially live on the same food and occupy the same type of water, but there are some important differences. Rainbows are capable of faster growth than browns and are usually more voracious feeders and much more liberal takers of anglers' flies and lures, all the more so when they are newly released after being reared in a hatchery. This means you don't need as large a stock of rainbow trout to turn a lake into a productive fishery as you do browns, which endears the fish to fishery managers as well as to anglers. Without the obliging rainbow trout, anglers would have to endure many more fruitless days and blank catch returns.

Since the rainbow was first introduced from the United States in the early 20th century, it has become the no 1 commercial trout in the UK, as it has across much of Europe and in many

Above: *A brown trout in a chalk-stream lie*

other countries of the world. It helps that the rainbow has a better tolerance of high temperatures and impure water than the brown, and is less dependent on mountain-fed streams. There are many places around the world, such as much of South Africa, the Far East and the North Island of New Zealand, which have proved a shade too warm for brown trout but where the rainbow has thrived.

The rainbow however has proved much less successful at establishing itself naturally in European waters than the brown. Rainbows are constantly escaping from managed fisheries, yet they almost invariably disappear. Only in a couple of rivers in the Peak District, the Derbyshire Wye and the Dove, have rainbows managed to naturalise themselves in Britain.

The Trout's Environment

The trout is superbly well-tuned to its environment. No other fish, perhaps no other creature, has managed to adapt to and dominate so many different habitats, from peaty mountain streams to sluggish lowland rivers, vast lakes and reservoirs and estuaries. With the helping hand of man over the last century and a half, both brown and rainbow trout have been distributed far beyond their original homes and may now be fished for in most countries of the world, from China to the Falklands, from India to the USA and Canada, southern and eastern Africa, Iceland, the Far East and Australasia. In all these countries the trout has quickly learned to feed on the available invertebrate life and to avoid most natural predators, thanks to its speed and power, its capacity for rapid growth and its ability to become almost invisible when danger threatens.

Water – The Trout's Element

The nature of water has a profound effect on the size and behaviour of all trout. The alkaline waters of chalk

streams and limestone-fed rivers are rich in minerals, supporting an abundance of plant life, which in turn nourish the creatures on which the fish live, so trout that live here tend to be plump and muscular. Acid waters on the other hand are often barren and infertile. Few plants thrive in these conditions, and the fish there will be small and agile, like the wild brown trout found in the rushing, upland waters of the Scottish highlands.

The quality of water can be measured on the pH (potential of hydrogen) scale, 0 representing extreme acidity and 14 alkalinity – 7 is a neutral solution. Brown trout thrive in water somewhere between 5.5 and 8.5. Spring-fed chalk streams provide a near perfect balance, with conditions ideal for both trout and flyfishers. The water in them tends to be crystal clear, having been filtered through the chalk, and as rainwater readily drains away into the underlying rock, their water levels remain constant and they can be fished throughout the season. These mineral-rich waters encourage prolific plant growth, which supports the many insects living there, but in high summer excessive weed growth may block the free flow of water.

Chalk streams require a degree of management to maintain open channels for feeding fish while still providing enough shelter to protect them from their predators. Trout in these waters grow strong and healthy, but with an abundance of food available to them, they can sometimes be difficult to catch.

Wild, rocky, rain-fed rivers offer a completely different environment, not just for trout, but for all the other creatures that live there. Their waters flow over impermeable, hard rocks which support little plant life. With fewer opportunities for food, the wily trout in these waters can be more ready takers, and the sport is all the more exciting for it.

Rain-fed rivers are subject to spates, rising and falling suddenly as the weather dictates, and they can be dangerous for the flyfisher. Fishing a spate river requires care and attention. You must always ensure that there is a safe way back to the bank in case the river rises suddenly.

So the size and the weight of brown trout depend mainly on the rivers in which they live and the food they produce. Those in bleak, upland rain-fed streams will be small and lean, whilst those which enjoy life in fertile chalk steams grow fast and can weigh several pounds. Sea trout feeding on the rich harvest of the ocean, as we shall see in later chapters, can reach enormous weights, 10-15 pounds or more being not uncommon.

The Fish's Window

Before you try to present a dry fly effectively, it's useful to understand the nature of the trout's vision. A trout's eyes are on the sides of its head, so its binocular vision is quite limited, but its field of monocular vision is relatively wide, enabling it to readily detect danger from predators. There is, however, a blind spot behind the fish, which can be used to great advantage by the dry flyfisher casting upstream. Here stealth and the lack of detection is vital.

When light rays enter water, which is a denser medium than air, they refract or bend upwards, presenting a displaced

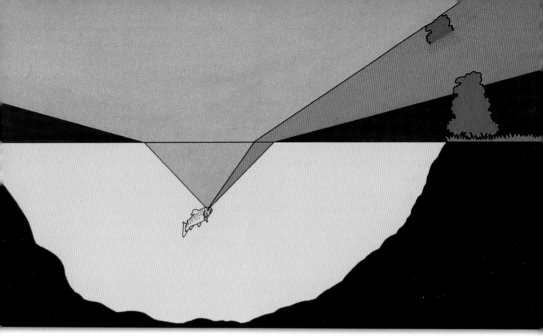

image to the eye. The extent of the displacement depends on the angle at which the rays meet the water. An object seen immediately above the fish is seen in its true location, while the further it moves to the edge of its circle of vision, the more displaced the object appears. Rays meeting the water at an angle of less than 10° cannot penetrate it at all, so the trout can see nothing below this angle. This is the main reason you should crouch low as you approach the river bank.

The area of water through which the fish can see clearly – the fish's window – is circular, and will be larger or smaller depending on how deep the fish is lying. Around this circle the water surface appears to the fish like a mirror which reflects the river bed. Trout no doubt rely on indentations in this mirror to recognise potential food items as they float by on the current. The shape and size of this indentation will appear to change as it moves from the mirror towards the circular window above the fish, but by then, the instinct to feed has often driven the fish to rise to take it.

The window effect works in favour of the angler for trout lying in wide, shallow glides and flats, as their window is severely restricted and it's often possible to watch the fish from the bank without detection. In deep, narrow stretches it's a different matter – stick your head over the bank and every fish within range will know you are there. And because the water is deep, you may not even see them fleeing for cover.

Colonel E W Harding, in his book, The Flyfisher and the Trout's Point Of View (1931), an important work on the subject, showed how:

"… the trout lying in wait with an upward gaze below a smooth surface is enabled to watch the reflection of the approaching nymph in the mirror made by the surface beyond the window through which he can see – and how, in order to keep the reflection in view of his upward gaze he has to come to the surface to meet the actual nymph as it and its reflection come together."

Understanding the trout's window is important to the dry fly angler, as there are several points to be learned from it. By crouching low on the bank, the angler can stay within the trout's blind spot, so as not to alarm it. This underlines the importance of casting your line as delicately as possible so that it falls lightly on the water. If the line slaps onto the surface it will create a flash in the mirror and create vibrations audible to the fish, which will invariably frighten them and put them down.

You need to be very careful too when lifting the line in preparation for the next cast. It may look delicate to you above the surface, but to the trout, a fly line being dragged through the "mirror" creates a massive disturbance and will again alarm the fish.

By the time your fly drifts over the fish's window it will be silhouetted against the sky with all its colour bleached out, so shape and size of the fly can often be more important than its colouring. Most important of all, avoid any unnatural drag caused by the fly. It shows up very clearly in the mirror and will again disturb the fish. The fly must drift naturally and smoothly on the current, and above all it must never skate across the surface of the water – unless you are trying to imitate a terrestrial insect.

The Food of the Trout

Natural Fly Life

A trout's diet is made up principally of the many invertebrates which live and breed on or close to water. Trout are avaricious and opportunistic predators, feeding on any aquatic life that becomes available as the seasons change.

However, despite their catholic tastes, at certain times of the year trout can become very particular in their feeding habits, often choosing to focus on only one group of insects at a time. If aquatic life in the river is abundant, they can become very selective, choosing a precise moment in a specific insect's short life cycle on which to feed, and then feeding on it voraciously. During a mayfly hatch they will often look at nothing but the hatching fly.

Trout are extremely territorial, but like any animal they use no more energy than they have to in order to obtain food. They will adopt different lies in a river depending on whether they are feeding or resting and on the height of the water, but they will usually have favourite feeding lies which they will defend against smaller fish. While trout will spend most of their time hovering in the current waiting to intercept aquatic insects such as olives, mayflies, sedges and chironomids (gnats), they will also forage around in weed beds picking up nymphs and snails, root around in the gravel in search of stonefly larvae or pick off terrestrial insects blown onto the water from surrounding fields and bank-side trees. Ants, alder flies, daddy-long-legs, caterpillars and moths all add to their rich and varied diet. Larger fish may adopt a fish-feeding habit, particularly in lakes.

Stories abound of the great and abundant fly hatches of the past. Unfortunately, in recent times there has been a gradual decline in the populations of many of Britain's indigenous fly species. Of the four main groups of aquatic insects of interest to the flyfisher, three, the mayflies (Ephemeroptera), the caddis flies (Trichoptera) and the stoneflies (Plecoptera) are all showing serious declines in their numbers. The Southern Iron Blue, once abundant throughout the UK has seen numbers decline by as much as 80% in recent times, and the Blue-Winged Olive and the mayfly species have all seen numbers dramatically fall.

At each and every stage of their life cycles, insects provide a vital link in the aquatic food chain, whether as larvae, pupae, emerging adults or egg-laying spinners, and their decline mirrors the decline in birds and butterflies, as well as the health of our wild trout populations.

River systems and the species they support are extremely sensitive to environmental change, and their condition is a good indication of the state of our natural environment as a whole. Freshwater invertebrates play a vital role in supporting the health and vitality of all our rivers and streams, and their declining numbers reflect these ecological and climactic changes.

There is considerable debate about why this has happened. Pollution from pesticides, herbicides and fertilisers and the run-off from surrounding farmland into our river systems must be partly responsible. Drainage and abstraction has dried out many water meadows and wetlands, so pollutants become more concentrated as they leach into the rivers. Alterations to river courses, for whatever reason, change the character of natural riverbanks and result in the loss of shallow bankside habitats. Soil erosion silts up the river beds, preventing plant growth and starving the river of the sanctuaries required for insect larvae to grow and develop. Acid rain, although less of a problem than it was, can drive the pH levels in some rivers down until the water no longer supports a viable invertebrate fauna. Anything lower than 5.5 and plant life struggles to survive.

Left: *Natural mayfly*

Factor in the colonization of non-native invasive species of insects and the fact that climate change has increased river water temperatures by, in places, as much as 3°C, and then consider that the populations of fish-eating birds such as cormorants, mergansers and goosanders have dramatically increased, and it's a wonder that anything survives in our rivers and streams at all.

Fortunately many aquatic creatures can be extremely resilient and able to manage to adapt to any changes in the environment. They need to be in order to survive. As a flyfisher, you need to adapt too, and to be keenly vigilant to the changes occurring in our rivers. A basic understanding of entomology and a keen eye to help identify the various insect orders and the various stages throughout their development will greatly enhance your ability to catch fish.

There are four key orders of insect which should be of interest to the flyfisher.

Mayflies (Ephemeroptera)

The word Ephemeroptera comes from the Greek meaning "day long" or "short lived". Mayflies are part of a group of some of the oldest insects ever recorded. There are some 2000 species of mayfly world wide, but in Great Britain the common mayfly (Ephemeroptera danica) is perhaps the most familiar to the dry fly angler. Mayflies are an important part of the trout's early summer diet in the clear, nutrient-rich, alkaline chalk streams of southern England, hatching in abundance from May onwards, but in other areas they form only a small part of their overall intake.

Mayflies belong to a group known as the upwinged flies, due to the elegant way in which they hold their wings vertically when at rest. Keen flyfishers and fly tiers are very familiar with the Iron Blue, the March Brown, the Pale Watery and the many and varied olives. The Mayfly is the largest of the group, and when the hatch is on, flyfishers will be out in their droves fishing with their dry imitations.

Late May and early June used to be known, rather disparagingly, as "duffer's fortnight", but in truth mayfly fishing is rarely easy. Much has been written about the tactics and techniques required to master the art of fishing with upwinged flies, and it became something of a cult among the fishing élite in the late nineteenth century. It requires a keen eye and an appreciation of entomology to be successful.

The development stages of most upwinged flies are very similar; the eggs are laid on or in the water, where they slowly sink before evolving into small nymphs, which burrow in the gravel and mud on the river bed and forage for food in the nutrient-rich rotting vegetation found there. The developing nymphs moult regularly as they grow in size over a period of between one and three years, all the while hiding away as best they can from predators. When they are ready to hatch, normally between mid-May and the first week in June, they produce small pockets of air around their bodies to aid buoyancy, then emerge from the safety of the river bed and swim to the surface. At this stage they are extremely vulnerable to feeding trout. As they reach the surface, they hang helplessly, suspended in the surface film waiting to hatch. Many are stillborn or get stuck at this stage, providing easy pickings, and trout have been known to target these exclusively.

When the time is right, the nymphal case splits open and the newly-hatched duns, or sub-imagos, emerge to rest on the water, with short legs and tails and pale, dull wings with soft brown veins. As soon as their wings dry, they fly away into the surrounding trees and bushes, where they wait until once again their backs split open, they shed their cases and the new flies emerge, completing their miraculous metamorphosis into adults.

Now they are known as spinners, or imagos. Male spinners are smaller and darker than the females and easily recognisable by the long tails that grow during the transformation from dun to adult and by their large eyes. The male spinners swarm in their courtship display dance, dipping and swooping about the surface until they can mate with the female, and then, rather sadly, they die. The females lay their eggs on the water, and then fall exhausted, and then they too die. Dead and dying spinners float along on the current, providing an inexhaustible, if temporary, supply of food for the waiting fish.

You can imitate the mayfly at all stages of its life cycle; with a nymph imitation during its nymphal stage and a dry fly once it has become a winged insect. You can imitate it as every subtle change occurs in its transformation from nymph to freshly-hatched dun and to adult spinner, and fly tiers have produced an array of patterns to match every stage. Not all mayflies are the same. They vary in character depending on the rivers they inhabit, and adapt accordingly.

Observing colour and size of insects is important, but matching the natural movement of your fly is critical. This is more important in deceiving the trout than anything else. Rather than be a slave to imitation, it's more important to identify exactly which species of upwing the fish are choosing to feed on and try to match its silhouette and movement. No matter how immaculate your imitation is, if it moves unnaturally, or if the fish are feeding on something else, your chances of catching one will be very slim.

Trout are likely to be less choosy at the beginning of the hatch before they have got their eye in, and you may be able to get away with more rough-and-ready approximations of the natural fly at this time, especially the emergers and newly-hatched duns, although they can become schooled quite quickly. As they begin to gorge on spent spinners, they can become extremely wary of any poor imitations presented to them by the flyfisher.

Other upwinged flies of interest to the angler are the members of the Baetidae family, flies such as the Iron Blue, the Pale Watery and some of the olives. They can be difficult to fish in their nymphal stages, but short, twitching movements will give the illusion of life and may induce a take. Try the Gold Ribbed Hare's Ear, fished wet, or just as the hatch begins, try the much favoured all-purpose Pheasant Tail Nymph. Not all upwings lay their eggs on the water; some, like the Iron Blue, crawl into the water and lay directly onto reeds, subsurface vegetation, partly submerged rocks and the like. It can often be more productive to fish these patterns as spent spinners on the surface.

The Large Dark Olive can be spotted very early in the season and in the autumn when it's colder and there are fewer insects around. Hatches can occur quite suddenly, often when there is a subtle change in the weather, and will not last very long, so you will need to be vigilant. If you like fishing at these times of the year, try a Pheasant Tail Nymph, or the very dark green Large Dark Brown Olive fished dry. Almost any of the olive patterns will do, as there is comparatively little insect life available and hungry trout will not be too selective.

As the weather becomes milder, look out for hatches of Medium Olives and Iron Blues, and then, from the middle to the end of May, if you are lucky enough to have the fishing then, prepare for the mayfly hatch.

The Pale Watery, a name encompassing a small group of pale upwings, can be found hatching throughout the day in British rivers during the summer months. Fish the nymphs, again with a standard Pheasant Tail or similar, but because the female spinners crawl down into the water to lay their eggs, they are best fished as they crawl back out onto the surface after egg laying.

The tiny Caenis, known as the 'angler's curse', is the smallest member of the upwing family. It hatches in great white clouds and can be difficult to imitate, but if you want to try, put on the smallest little white fly you can manage – though sometimes a big white fly will deceive the trout, perhaps because they think it's a whole bundle of caenis!

Caddis Flies (Trichoptera) (also known as sedge flies)

Caddis flies, or sedge flies, proliferate throughout the world, with some 200 species recognised in Britain. They can be found in most of our freshwater habitats and are often extremely numerous. Their life cycle consists of

four stages: egg, larva, pupa and finally the winged adult stage, the whole cycle taking, on average about a year to complete. Female adults lay their eggs either on the water surface or just beneath it, after which the eggs sink down to the riverbed and settle on weeds until they are ready to hatch as larvae.

All stages in the life cycle of the caddis fly are important to feeding trout, and therefore of interest to the flyfisher. The larval stage of most species is instantly recognisable. The grub builds a hard case around its body, leaving its head and legs protruding so that it can move around and feed. This acts as camouflage and affords a certain amount of protection from its predators, although trout will seek them out and devour them, hard cases and all. Their cases vary in construction, depending on the species and where they live, but building materials will often include sand and small gravel, small particles of vegetation, even twigs and pine needles. As the larvae slowly fatten up, many will adapt their cases to cope with changes in river flows, adding more weight as necessary. A successful imitation needs to be weighted so that it can be fished very slowly along the riverbed. Remember too that larvae will be larger than at any other stage in their life cycle, so you can fish with a reasonably big imitation fly.

When the larva reaches maturity, after about a year, it seals itself into its case in preparation for its transformation into the pupal stage. This phase is relatively brief. When the time is right, it wriggles free from the river bed and surfaces to hatch as an adult. It is now at its most vulnerable, firstly as it rises

Above: *Sedge Fly*

Left: *Caddis grub underwater*

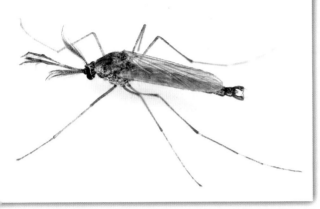

through the water, many getting trapped in the surface film as they drift along on the current, and then as it struggles to get airborne. Caddis flies are not dissimilar in appearance to moths, with four wings folded back over their bodies, but they are instantly recognisable by their long antennae.

The adults mate among the bankside vegetation and then the females return to the river, more often than not in the evenings, to lay their eggs, some crawling into the water, some diving deep down to the river bed, others choosing to lay their eggs on the surface. As they skitter about, their movements become particularly inviting to trout. Winged adults mix with new hatchlings and you can be sure of some good sport, especially in the last hour of the day. Look out for plenty of action on the surface as the trout get over-excited at the possibility of missing out on a feeding frenzy. You can fish for them with both dry flies and winged wet flies now. When fishing the dry fly, it pays to imitate their sudden jerking, panicky movements as accurately as possible, twitching your fly to resemble the naturals. Try to identify the particular hatch, and take note of the flies' silhouette and wing size, more so than perhaps their colour. Remember that trout can very easily become selective and focused on one species.

Early in the season, the Grannom is one of the first sedges to show. You will find them on many waters, from chalk streams to remote and wild upland streams, and unlike many caddis flies, they hatch during the day. Look out for them in the late mornings. There are many caddis imitations you can try, depending on where you fish, but a Wickham's Fancy is a good reliable pattern at this time on most rivers.

Chironomids

The order of Diptera has evolved into one of the largest and most diverse insect groups in the world, including many familiar species. Mosquitoes,

THE FOOD OF THE TROUT

crane flies (daddy-long-legs), house flies and midges are all members of this vast family of two-winged insects. The most interesting group for the flyfisher is the Chironomidae or midge family, of which there are some four hundred different species, all sharing the same life cycle pattern. Considered to be one of the least important aquatic insects to the river flyfisher, midges are a major food source for trout in stillwaters, and well known to the stillwater angler. Here they'll feed on "buzzers" or duck flies, as fishermen know them (mallard ducklings often feed on them), more than on any other insect, especially when the pupae are rising to the surface. Over the years stillwater anglers have developed all manner of techniques to catch them. An awareness of their value as a food item for river trout, especially during the pupal stage, is very useful to the river angler.

Adult midges mate on the wing on warm evenings throughout the year. The females lay their eggs on the surface of the water, and as they begin to hatch the larvae slowly sink to the safety of the river bed, where they can hide in the mud and feed on decaying vegetation. Huge populations of chironomids inhabit most

of our still and slow-moving waters, and they have the capacity to survive in most aquatic habitats where there is a reasonably stable riverbed, gentle currents and a healthy weed growth.

After a year or so in the river, the larvae shed a final layer of skin and develop into pupae, this stage lasting no more than a day or two. Then, when conditions are right, they swim up to the surface, where they will lie just under the surface film before shedding their final skins to emerge as winged adults. Hatching times vary, depending on the species. Unlike the mayfly and other ephemerid flies, most emerge from their shucks and take off instantly.

Fortunately for the trout, many get trapped in the surface film, and these insects, together with the rising pupae, provide a veritable feast for hungry fish. They will feed on chironomids throughout the season and at all stages in their metamorphosis and it can be a big mistake to ignore them. Trout will often favour them above much larger flies and have been know to feed on them to the exclusion of almost everything else. When buzzers and sedges are hatching together on a summer's evening, buzzer imitations may take fish after fish while

LITTLE BOOK OF **FLY FISHING** FOR TROUT   23

sedge patterns are ignored.

When you're trying to imitate the pupae, remember that like most insect species, midges decrease in size throughout their development; the larvae are larger than the pupae, which in turn are larger than the adults.

Chironomid larvae can be difficult to imitate, as their colours are subtle and variable, but bloodworms, the bright red midge larvae, can be imitated reasonably successfully. They should be fished close to the bottom with a very slow retrieve, stopping every now and again to simulate resting creatures. Wire ribbing to suggest the nine body segments of the natural, with a bit of sparkle from seal's fur to give the illusion of translucence, may help. Like many waterborne insects, during both the larvae and the pupa stages, chironomids produce small amounts of air which inflate the pupae to enable them to ascend through the water, and it can be worthwhile including a translucent material in your fly dressings to imitate this colouring.

The pupal stage is when the midge is at its most vulnerable, but it is also when it is at its most attractive to feeding fish. Midge pupae have a number of distinctive features, including segmented bodies forming a curved comma-shaped profile and a distinctive bulbous thorax with white filaments which should be copied in your fly pattern. They can be found in a vast array of colours, including shades of tan, green and olive, but black or black and red artificials are usually effective. Buzzers can be tied in a variety of patterns, including popular variations like the Black Buzzer and the Black Hatching Pupa Buzzer.

The hatch can take place at all times of the day, but in the spring midge pupae often surface in the mornings and trout will start to feed on them by the middle of the day. At other times of the year mornings and evenings will be a better time to catch them. As they rise up from the river bed, the little pupae wriggle and kick their way to the surface, and if you are attempting to imitate them at this stage, gently twitching your retrieve can be very successful. On warm evenings, thousands will sometimes hatch, many lying horizontally just below the surface, waiting for the time when their backs split open and the newly formed adults crawl out, break free and fly away. Trout like to feed on them in the safety of the deep water, just as they begin to swim to the surface, but they will also take them

Above: *Stonefly*

just under the surface.

Watch for the way the fish are feeding. If they are coming up just below the surface and sipping down the flies, or you spot them as their backs break the surface, gently porpoising as they take in the trapped pupae, then try fishing for them on a floating line with a very long leader keeping your fly dipping in, or just below the surface film. If it's a particularly prolific hatch, consider putting on a slightly larger imitation so that it stands out amongst many thousands of naturals.

Once airborne, chironomids concentrate in large clouds away from the river under trees and close to buildings; you can hear the sound of their buzzing (hence the name) as they gather in great swarms before mating in the air. After mating, the females return to the river, skating across the water and dipping below the surface to lay their eggs, a good time for the angler to consider imitating the natural and catching a fish on the dry fly.

Adult chironomids have long slender bodies, similar to the pupae, with a pair of flat wings laid back over the body when not in flight. The Teal and Black is a very useful chironomid wet fly imitation for the river fisherman and the Parachute Buzzer is a very useful dry fly pattern. It doesn't bear a great resemblance to the natural, but it has a small vertical fluorescent wing which enables you to keep an eye on it as you fish it.

Stoneflies (Plecoptera)

Stoneflies are commonly found on tumbling upland rivers and streams where the water is well oxygenated and the riverbed is made up of gravel and stones. In this harsh environment, the robust stonefly is a valuable food source for wild brown trout. There are some thirty species in Britain, and they are instantly recognisable by their two short prominent tails, in contrast to the three tails found on most upwinged flies.

Depending on the species, the nymphs crawl around on the river bed, feeding on decaying vegetation for two to three years. During their nymphal stage they will moult many times before seeking out shallower water in readiness to hatch. Trout will root among the

stones, digging them out and feeding on them, but at this stage it can be difficult to present a fly that looks convincing without getting snagged up on the bottom. When stoneflies hatch, any time from the end of March to the end of June, the adults look very similar to the nymphs, brown and green in colour, some with yellowish underbellies, except that the adults carry hard, shiny wings that fold back over their bodies when resting. They are generally poor flyers, preferring to creep around and mate on dry land, but when the time comes, the females fly back to the river and lay their eggs in small batches, dipping into the water, or creeping over the surface. Trout feed on them at two stages in their life cycle: during the nymphal stage, and when the females lay their eggs, and as spent flies sink below the surface.

Terrestrials

There are many terrestrial insects which contribute to the trout's varied diet. The grubs typically hatch from eggs on dry land, and as adults some find themselves caught on the wind and swept out onto the water, while others simply fall from bankside trees and shrubs. Many terrestrial species suffer this fate and end up as food for hungry fish.

Crane flies or daddy-long-legs are a familiar sight on many of our rivers, especially our chalk streams later in the summer, when they can be blown onto the water from nearby fields, their long dangling legs dancing about on the water surface. Many find themselves caught up in the surface film, helpless and unable to escape, and trout will be quick to take advantage of these poor creatures. They can offer great sport to the flyfisher. Some modern daddy-long-legs patterns are very realistic and should be fished dry, their bodies and trailing legs resting in the surface film, sometimes inert, sometimes as if they are struggling to break free. If the trout are nipping at them but not taking them, it may be because the fly is sitting too high on the water. Make sure the fly sits down on the water. You can also try dapping for them over rippled water, holding the rod tip high and letting the fly dance across the surface. Trout willing to take a dapped daddy-long-legs will give you excellent sport.

Tiny black gnats with their swept-back wings appear in abundance on our rivers in the warmer months. Their larger relative the hawthorn fly, with its pale grey wings and trailing legs, is an early season fly, but when it hatches it can be devoured in huge numbers if the trout take to them. Small flying black ants will often be swept up on the breeze and land on the water in large numbers. Caterpillars and beetles may fall from overhanging bankside trees and plants and provide an excellent protein-rich food source for fish throughout the season. Other winged insects such as moths can often lose their way and fall to the water. So you can see, it's very important not to underestimate the importance of terrestrial insects as a major part of the overall diet of our river trout. You can imitate them one way or another throughout the season and at most times of the day.

If you see fish sitting tight under the bank in the shade of overhanging branches, and you believe they are feeding on terrestrials but are refusing your fly, it can sometimes be worth "plopping" a fly onto the water to simulate the insect falling in. If they still refuse it, try putting on a larger fly or a different terrestrial pattern. Don't always be in too much hurry to cast to a rising trout in this situation. Give it time to drop back into its lie and digest its last bite, and then cast well upstream and let the fly drift down over it. It may do the trick.

Tackle and Methods

One of the great joys of fly fishing for brown trout is that you are free to wander the banks of the river and indulge your spirit as a hunter, in search of a quarry you can take home and eat. This calls for stealth, skill and patience, as well as the ability to make the most of every chance that arises. You need to understand something of the natural world around you as you explore the river, and to experiment in your efforts to catch your fish.

At its simplest, you require little more than a rod, a reel with the right line, some leader material and a few flies. However, flyfishers like kit, and most of us will take a jacket or waistcoat with a spare spool of leader, some clippers, a priest; floatant if you're dry fly fishing; a pair of Polaroids and, if conditions demand it, maybe a wading stick. You will usually also need a net, one which can be carried on your person while fishing – unless you are using a bank net of the kind use by reservoir anglers, which has a long spiked pole enabling you to thrust it into the mud of the lake bed and leave it there to stake your spot (unless this is against the rules).

Carry as little as you can. The freedom to move around, unencumbered, is essential if you're to become a part of the natural environment, unthreatening in presence of the fish you hope to catch.

Choosing your tackle from the vast array of rods, reels and lines now available on the market is no easy matter.

Rods and reels come in all sizes, and fly lines in a baffling array of densities and profiles. There are some who still like to fish with traditional tackle, and there is something magical about playing a wild brown trout on an old split cane rod, but beautiful as cane rods are, carbon-fibre rods are far more efficient and are now used almost exclusively for fly rods. This material is without doubt the best material for the job because of its lightness, rapid recovery from bending and durability.

Fly Rods and Reels

The most important factor with any rod is that it must be matched to a suitably rated fly line. All modern rods are marked with an AFTM (Association of Fishing Tackle Manufacturers) number which denotes the line most suited to the rod; the higher the number, the heavier the line. The AFTM number is based on the head weight of the line – the weight of the portion you cast with – and the rod and line should balance

each other for the best performance of both. Unlike other methods of fishing, spinning for instance, it's the line that loads the rod. If it's too light, there will be insufficient flex in the rod and it will be difficult to cast effectively. If too heavy, you will risk breaking the rod. Most modern rods are, however, made with a degree of tolerance, so if you are fishing a small river and don't need to throw out a long line, its possible to fish a slightly heavier line for ease of casting, without damaging the rod.

All manufactures produce a range of rod styles, and many have different "actions"; one rod may be marketed as having a "slow" or traditional action while another will be described as having a "fast" action, and there are many in between. These terms describe the steepness of the curve. A fast rod is relatively stiff in the butt and middle with most of its flexing at the top, while a slower, easier-action rod bends in a more circular shape.

Generally speaking, slow action rods are softer and a little easier to cast. They tend to cast a wider loop and present the fly more delicately, but sometimes accuracy can be more difficult, especially if there's a breeze. Fast action rods are stiffer and more powerful, forming a tight loop that's ideal for cutting through the wind and for casting longer distances, but this is not necessarily important on a small river in the summertime. Stillwater

flyfishers like them, especially if the rod is longer and distance is important, but for river fishing, an all–round medium action is ideal. It's less tiring than a fast action rod and more forgiving when it comes to any inconsistencies in the angler's casting technique.

The length of your rod will depend mainly on where you choose to fish. A short rod of 7-8 feet is handy where casting room is restricted, while a rod of 9-10 feet gives more control at a distance and when manoeuvring your line over bankside vegetation. Ten feet is a good length for fishing lakes and the larger rivers. The ideal set-up for most river situations is a nine foot #5 rod, good for throwing a decent length of line, but short enough to cast with accuracy.

The fly reel's main function for the small river fisherman is to store line and backing. It is not used when casting, or to animate or to retrieve the flies, and in most cases on small waters it is not necessary to play a fish from the reel, though for sea-trout fishing, where you are likely to hook a powerful fish capable of making long runs, this is almost essential. A modern, strong, lightweight alloy reel is all that's needed. The better ones tend to have sealed drag systems, making them virtually maintenance free, and large arbours which allow the line to be recovered quickly. Most reel spools have holes in the sides which keep the weight down and help to dry the fly line quickly, and prevent coil memory when the line is stored after use. Bear in mind that you will probably need spare spools to carry different lines, as removing one line from a reel and winding a new one on is far too troublesome a process to be carried out while you're fishing unless you have to. Beyond that, it's a matter of taste and cost, and finding a reel that suits you.

There are some very beautiful rods and reels on the market, hand-crafted and finished to perfection. Modern reels made using state-of-the-art materials are wonderful feats of engineering, and the rod maker's art has never been finer, but spending a fortune on rods and reels won't make you a better fisherman. If cost is no object, then it's a pleasure to own some of these beautifully-crafted tools, but if you have budgetary constraints, the most important items in your tackle bag are your lines, and you should buy the very best that you can afford.

Fly Lines

Fly fishing is very different from most other methods of fishing in that it requires the angler to throw a "fly", which by definition has little or no weight to it, a considerable distance through the air, and the only way to do this is to use the weight of the fly line. It's the line that loads the rod and pulls the fly through the air, not the lure or the bait.

Modern fly lines are made by coating a strong, braided inner core with layers of different plastic, depending on whether it's a floating, intermediate or sinking line. Like the rod, the fly line is rated with an AFTM code, and provided the two are matched correctly and the correct length of line is aerialised, the line should cast perfectly. It's a simple system to follow; the first letters represent the lines profile; DT for double taper, WF for weight-forward, etc. The number next to it represents the weight of the first 10 yards of line, often marked with a # symbol, and the last letter indicates whether the line is a floating (F) sinking (S) or intermediate (I) line. There are many other variations, so a typical code might read WF6F, denoting a weight-forward, size 6 floating line.

There are a multitude of variations on these lines on the market to suit most river conditions, including various densities of sinking lines, sinking tips, shooting heads and spey lines. Generally speaking you will need a heavier line to cast a heavy fly, such as a lure or weighted nymph. More than ever, you need to research the market or consult your tackle supplier so that you buy the best lines to suit your fishing.

For many years flyfishers favoured double taper-fly lines. They are ideal for casting shorter lines, turn over smoothly, present the fly delicately, and have the added advantage that they can be reversed as one end begins to fray, extending the life of the line. They were always considered to be easier to roll cast than weight-forward lines, and in many ways they are still hard to beat. However, fly lines have undergone a transformation over the past few years, and manufacturers have worked hard to improve on the old traditional profiles.

Weight-forward lines, long popular on reservoirs, have been specifically developed for the river fisherman. They have long front tapers which graduate down to a fine tip, long bellies and often integrated running lines, and they are easy to cast and are ideal for delicate fly presentation. Given that on most trout streams you rarely need to cast more than 10 to 12 meters, some of the belly on a weight-forward line will remain within the rod rings, so the rod loads powerfully and casting is effortless.

Weight-forward lines are available in a vast range of densities and weights, and in an assortment of colours depending on the manufacturer. Most have colour changes to indicate exactly where the optimum loading point is – a useful guide – but a proficient caster can choose how much line is needed outside the rod tip and cast accordingly.

It doesn't matter much what colour the line is. All the manufactures offer their own variations, but trout seem not to be too concerned about colour. What does scare them is the shadow of a fly line flashing over their heads, glinting in the sunlight, and slashing down on the water in front of them. Fewer false casts with a matt line and a delicate presentation will help you to catch more fish.

A shooting head is a tapered length of 10-12m of fly line which is attached to a thin shooting line. They are designed entirely for long-range casting, and there is very little call for them for river trout fishing, or indeed for most lake fishing. They are mainly useful for reservoir fishermen, where long casts to reach far-off fish can be a distinct advantage.

Leaders

When choosing a leader, make sure it's strong enough to take control of a decent fish in the sort of water you'll be fishing. If you are fishing a chalk stream, and expect to catch decent-sized trout, you might use a leader of around 4-5 pounds. In a wild-rain fed river where the fish are small, you might get away with something lighter, but only if you have room to play the fish; snaggy water with boulders or fallen tree branches will require plenty of pressure to stop a trout, and fish in wild waters have less time to notice the leader in the first place.

Fishing too fine and losing fish to breaks in your leader is unforgivable. Provided you have the space, your leader should be very roughly the same length as your rod, tapered, and attached to a small length of uniform diameter tippet material, to which the fly is tied. That way, you can replace the tippet when it gets too short while still keeping the same leader. Tapered leaders are not essential, however, particularly in the rougher waters of upland rivers.

If you find the leader difficult to turn over in the final cast, make it shorter at the end where it connects to the fly line. It's a fine point (forgive the pun) whether you use traditional nylon, fluorocarbon or copolymer materials, but when fishing chalk streams, copolymer leaders, which are softer, work better for dry fly fishing and fluorocarbon, which is denser, may be better for nymph fishing. Ready-made leaders with loop-to-loop connectors are available from tackle shops, but you may prefer to connect them with a blood knot.

There are a number of knots flyfishers need to master. If you are unfamiliar with them, you should practise tying them well before you go down to the river. The key knots are the reel knot, for tying the backing to the spool; the loop to loop, for connecting the leader to the fly line; the blood knot, for tying together lengths of nylon and for making droppers; the water knot, another good knot for tying on droppers; the half blood knot, tucked or untucked; and the turle knot for tying the fly to the tippet. The turle is a better knot for larger flies.

There are others, and the printed page is not the ideal place to learn them. Many are illustrated on the internet, and you can pick them up as you need them, after which you need to practice.

Care and Conservation Methods

Catch and Release

The arguments for catch and release for river trout fishers are very different from those for the salmon angler. North Atlantic salmon populations are in decline in North America, Canada and Europe, and a catch–and–release policy is a highly effective conservation tool, playing an ever more vital role in many fishery management programs. It's not mandatory on all rivers, but increasingly salmon fishers are choosing to return their fish and in their own way contribute to the wider efforts to conserve this wonderful wild resource.

Catch and release on trout rivers rests more on the need for effective fishery management programmes to maintain a healthy population of wild brown trout at a time when the demand for fly fishing is at an all–time high. The practice of stocking rivers with reared fish, fertile and infertile, had become widespread as many fisheries struggled to replenish natural stocks and satisfy the demand from anglers and angling clubs, but current thinking suggests that domesticated, fertile fish can and do pose a risk to wild brown trout populations, greatly reducing the ability of the interbred progeny to survive in the wild. They may even affect the long–term future of the wild brown trout.

The Environment Agency has

announced that from 2015, all fisheries wanting to maintain reasonable levels of stock will be compelled to stock with either reared infertile females, (triploids), or fish that have been bred from native broodstocks, and reared under controlled regimes to ensure sustainability and a minimal impact of existing wild populations. This is a difficult process at best, but in theory it's a good idea; there will be less pressure on the natural wild fish, their numbers will improve over time and fewer of the more expensive triploids will need to be reared for release. Ideally, ongoing research, experimentation and habitat improvements should, in the end, result in strategies where native strains of trout are reared in suitable local environments and released back into the wild, but in the meantime, stocking with triploids means there are still plenty of fish for the angler to fish for.

You should always check the local rules on the rivers where you fish, and abide by them. Some will insist that you kill a certain number of stocked fish, but others will recognise that catch and release is no more than a way of continuing to fish for longer without exceeding your limit.

Barbless Hooks

The case for barbless hooks is a strong one, especially when it's considered as part of a catch and release strategy. The main advantage is that in most cases the hook can be easily removed without lifting the fish from the water, thereby limiting its levels of stress and the amount of time it's handled. Some flyfishers are concerned that they will lose more fish if they use barbless hooks, but in practice it seems to make little difference. With a firm strike, the hook will drive home, and provided you keep a tight line as you play your fish, there's no reason why it should get off. Barbless hooks invariably causes less damage, and if a fish has given you a great fight, when you finally bring it in, it will have suffered enough without then being lifted out of the water to remove the hook. Keep it in the water, gently slip the hook from its mouth and let it swim away.

Some commercial barbless hooks are too fine, but any hook can be made barbless. Simply crush the barb on a forged hook with a pair of pliers, and then, when a big trout takes it, you can play it with confidence, especially if you plan to release it. Black nickel hooks

Above: *A large sea trout about to be returned*

are ideal; they are difficult to spot in the sun and greatly reduce "flashing". If you are a keen fly-tier, consider making up a number of patterns with barbless hooks and try them. You may lose the odd fish, but you will be surprised how little difference it makes to your fishing, and how much better it is for the fish. It might be wise to use a stronger leader because you can be harder on your fish, play them for a shorter time and release them more quickly.

Mastering the Cast

There is a lot of mystique attached to casting a fly line, some of it apparently designed to intimidate rather than encourage the beginner. It's a mistake to be put off, for once you get the knack you will wonder what all the fuss was about.

As one of the great salmon fishers, Arthur Oglesby, said, "Good casting is not an art; it's merely a craft that can be learned." But it is a skill that needs to be mastered if you want to maximise your enjoyment as a flyfisher.

Spending time with a qualified casting instructor can pay huge dividends, especially if you visit them before any faults have developed in your technique. It doesn't matter whether you're a novice or a seasoned flyfisher, faults develop, and if you are not careful they become ingrained in what we think of as our "style". In fact, as often as not, it's simply bad technique. Faults can be extremely difficult to rectify once ingrained, but a good instructor will help to identify them and put you back on track.

Learning to Cast

The written word is not the best place to find good instruction. Nowadays there is a wealth of video tuition available to view on the internet, some of it good and some not so good, but it's worthwhile looking at what's available. However, time spent with

a good instructor offering one–to–one tuition will be of most value. It will teach you timing and muscle memory, and help you to realise that if you get it right, the rod will do most of the work for you.

New equipment, new techniques and new casting styles are being developed all the time and it will pay you to learn about them from a skilled instructor. There are many individuals and organisations with the necessary accreditations. You can easily find them through the internet. However, if for any reason you are unable to employ the services of an instructor, then pick up a shortish carbon fibre rod with a floating line, tie a small piece of wool to the leader and practise in the garden, in the park, wherever you can.

Good casting has nothing to do with brute force; it's all about timing, and developing an instinctive harmony between your rod, hand and eye. It's important to remember that the rod must do the work – that's what it's designed for. The most common mistake is that in our eagerness to throw a long

line, we put far too much effort into the cast. More than anything else, fly fishing, especially for the wily river trout, is all about delicate, accurate presentation, and how you place your fly on to the water will make all the difference as to whether or not you catch fish.

The Overhead Cast

The basic cast is the overhead cast, and it's a simple action. Begin by holding the rod comfortably, ideally with the thumb on top of the rod butt, or you may prefer to grip it with the V between your thumb and forefinger on top. It doesn't much matter provided your grip is not too firm and you feel comfortable. Start by pulling off 10-12 meters of line and laying it down in front of you, either on short grass or on the water. Now start the back cast with the rod tip down below the horizontal and the line taut in front of you. Bear in mind that all the action will take place on an imaginary vertical clock face.

Smoothly draw the line up, accelerating as you reach 12 o'clock. It will inevitably go back past that position, but you must never let it go beyond 2 o'clock. Then stop, and allow the line to extend well out air behind you and straighten out. Then, with an equally smooth forward cast, and keeping the rod vertical, look at where you want to position the fly and aim the line out well above it. Always aim at something deliberately – it's a good discipline to learn, and useful when targeting individual fish later on. Try to stop the rod at the ten o'clock position on the forward cast, and as the line tightens gently lower it to the water. Avoid any attempt to push the rod forward, as this will kill the "spring" in the rod and results

released. The hand travels only a short distance forward and backward. This short, forceful motion translates to the rod tip swinging through 90 degrees or so, sending the line forward, then backward, in a narrow loop which finally unfurls to release your line above the water. If you try too hard, or the rod swings too far forward or back and the line cannot keep up with it, the loop is destroyed and the line falls in a heap.

Try it, with nothing in your hand. You lift back slowly and deliberately, the wrist held firm, the forearm steadily gaining momentum, the action stopping never further back than at about one o'clock. There is then a fraction of a delay (only practice will tell you how long, but it's probably no more than a second) to allow the line to straighten behind before the forward stroke begins. Punch forward to apply the power, and the loop shoots forward.

Try not to hold your arm too high in a mistaken attempt to keep the line up. The extra few inches will make no difference – the line will stay up comfortably once you get the timing right. Practise flicking the rod to and fro on the lawn, and you'll soon realise just how little effort is involved in casting.

in a loss of power.

Never allow your wrist to bend on the back cast, as this will allow the rod to drop behind you and ruin the cast. The action is like pulling a punch – very tightly controlled, so you accelerate your hand, then brake it again, applying power to the rod during only a very short arc.

If you watch an efficient caster at work you will see that most of the bending happens at the elbow. The hand and wrist remain all of a piece throughout, the wrist hardly bending until the cast is

Right: *As the rod is punched forward, the left hand pulls the line down*

The Role of the Left Hand

Now to the left hand (assuming you are right handed), which is just as important as the rod-holding hand. Pinch the line in the fingers of the left hand between the reel and the bottom ring. As you raise the rod back, keep that hand down – do not be tempted to let your hand follow the rod butt as it goes back, as many beginners instinctively do. Keeping your hand down will draw line back through the rings as the rod is raised, adding to the speed of the back cast.

Now, when you punch the rod forward, drive the left hand down towards the ground at the same time. If you keep your left hand where it was, the rod will approach it on the forward cast and the distance between the butt ring and your left hand will sharply reduce. This will feed line back through the rings and waste most of the energy the rod has put into the cast – like drawing back a bowstring and then moving it back towards the bow before you release the arrow.

When your forward cast is approaching its full extent (only practice will tell you the right moment), simply

release the line from your left hand and the tip of your line should fall on the water about 10–12 yards away, with the leader and fly extended out beyond it. When you have got the hang of this, strip a couple of yards of line from the reel and allow it to hang between the reel and the left hand. Next time you release a cast, if you're doing it right, this extra line will shoot out as well. With practice and good timing, you should be

end of your first season. This is more than enough for most rivers, but longer casting can be very useful on lakes and reservoirs. To cast further than about 25 yards with ordinary fly tackle you will need to learn the double haul, in which the left hand plays a much bigger role – but that is a subject for more advanced tuition.

False casting should be avoided, other than to dry your fly. It makes you more visible and alarms the fish. However, there are many circumstances where you will need to be able to the false cast, such as drying your fly or changing direction.

False casting simply means following the forward cast with another back cast instead of letting go of the line and allowing the file to touch the water. Do it just enough times to dry your fly and when you're ready, release the line as before. Try to false cast away from the target and only in the final cast aim where you want to present the fly. Remember, you need just enough false casts to dry your fly and judge your distances, but not so many that it becomes an end in itself.

Bear in mind that a long cast doesn't necessarily mean you'll catch more fish, and bad presentation will invariably scare

able to persuade around five yards of line to fly out in addition to the line that's been in the air, giving you a cast of 15–20 yards. The line and leader will not straighten unless the line is being stopped at the reel, so if this is not happening, wind a little line back on until it does.

Don't expect to cast a long way at first – you will do well to cast 15 yards (rod butt to fly) the first time, gradually extending to perhaps 25 yards by the them away.

Finally, when your line has fished around on the current, draw it in slowly and you will see how the surface film of the water resists your pull slightly. This will automatically load the rod ready for your next cast. Try not to rip the line off the water, as this will disturb any fish resting close in to your bank.

Once you've mastered the basic overhead cast, you will know what it feels like to move the line through the air, letting the rod do the work with the minimum amount of effort. Now you can experiment with other casts. Much of your dry fly fishing will be from a crouching position, or on your knees, and this you will need to practise before you get to the river on an expensive fishing day. Try casting sideways, useful when under trees and overhanging branches. The danger here will be that the line drops on the back cast and catches behind you, but provided you keep the line up, the action is the same as the overhead cast. You will find it much harder to place the fly accurately with a side cast, but this will come with practice. Always remember to aim above the target and let the fly drop down delicately onto the water.

The Roll Cast

The roll cast is the next important cast to master. It's essential if there are trees, bushes or high banks behind you, and there's no room for a back cast. It's also useful when you need to bring sinking and intermediate lines up to the surface prior to casting. Start by lowering the rod tip, and then slowly lift it up to a point a little beyond the vertical. You can take your time with this. You'll find that a small loop is then laid in front of the rod on the water – remember, it's the drag of the water that loads the rod. Then, with a snap of the wrist, you punch the line out. There is no back cast. All the power is in the action of the wrist and the flex in the rod. Try not to push the hands forward. As with all casting, this will dissipate all the power and prevent the line from rolling out.

A final thought on casting; long casts look good and will impress your friends, but a long floating line lying on the water picks up all the little currents and eddies, and all these swirls risk imparting drag on your fly. It would be far better to exercise all your skills as a hunter, creep into a better position and cast a much shorter line. You'll be far more accurate,

present a much better fly, have less line drifting around on the water – and your fish will be better hooked.

The Retrieve

In river fishing you will often not need to pull in line to work the fly, but in stillwater fishing it can be very important. You can do this by 'stripping' – pulling the line back through the butt ring with your fingers, a foot or two at a time. A more precise technique is 'figure of eighting', a rotary motion of the hand in which you draw the line back an inch or two with the finger and thumb, then hook your middle and ring fingers over the line to draw back another couple of inches, then transfer this to the finger and thumb, and so on, creating a very slow and steady retrieve in which you never let go of the line – ideal for nymph fishing.

Above: *The figure of eight retrieve*

River Fishing

There is no more delightful branch of angling than casting a fly for wild trout in a clear, fast-flowing stream. Nowhere is the fly angler's art more finely developed, and nowhere is skill more richly rewarded.

The methods used to catch trout in these waters need to match the conditions. Trout streams vary enormously in size and character. At one extreme are the chalk streams of southern England, whose clear, alkaline waters produce prolific plant and fly life which enable the fish to grow big. At the other are the peaty, acidic torrents of the mountains of northern and western Britain and Ireland, where the trout are generally small but incomparably hard-fighting.

Chalk Stream Fishing

The Dry Fly

For many, casting a dry fly upstream on one of the famous spring-fed chalk streams represents the pinnacle of fly-fishing, and if an opportunity is offered, few flyfishers would turn it down. The expectation is that the trout will be fat and muscular, well fed on the abundance of insect life found in these crystal-clear waters. When they are feeding on surface flies and emergers, you can be sure of some exciting fishing. Dry fly fishing is by no means exclusive to the south - any river with a hatch of fly will offer great sport - but the intense

passion for the dry fly was born on the chalk streams of southern England, becoming something of a cult in the late nineteenth century.

A proliferation of books appeared on the subject. Famous angling writers such as F M Halford and George Selwyn Marryat, passionate and dedicated chalk

stream fishermen, laid down the lore, wisdoms which have endured to this day. Through their writing, they influenced the way in which fisheries were run, and their tactics and techniques were quickly adopted by ever-growing numbers of flyfishers. There wasn't always agreement between them all; Halford was something of a purist in his preoccupation with the dry fly and the need for exact imitation. He believed that the only decent and proper way to catch brown trout was to "fish up and fish fine", using exact imitations of naturals found in the river.

Marryat, his close friend and fishing companion for many years, was a keen supporter of Halford and influenced much of his work, but he had his

reservations when it came to Halford's exclusive methodology. Known as the "Prince of Flyfishers", and considered the finest chalk stream angler of his day, he was a keen amateur entomologist and an innovative fly tier, prepared to experiment with a range of new materials. He took a microscopic interest in the trout's diet, and through his observations went on to develope patterns with lighter dressing, specifically designed to float, which were extremely successful. But unlike his friend, he was just as happy to fish the wet fly on the rain-fed rivers of the north.

Many of their contemporaries disagreed with this rather evangelical approach, and were possibly much better flyfishers for it. Francis Francis, then angling editor of the Field and a regular companion of both of them, wrote:

"The judicious and perfect application of dry, wet and mid-water fly fishing stamps the finished flyfisher with the hallmark of efficiency".

G.E.M. Skues, although a few years younger, also went on to become one of the great angling writers of the time. He fished the same southern chalk streams, but later went on to challenge the dry fly orthodoxy. Through keen observation, he noted that trout would often start to feed on emerging nymphs just prior to their hatching, and would often gorge on them to the point where they were so full that they would ignore

Dry Flies

Iron Blue Dun

Lunn's Spent Gnat

Red Quill (Imitation of the blue winged olive)

Wickhams Fancy

Kite's Imperial

Tups Indispensible

March Brown

Large Dark Olive

Grannom

Pale Watery

Mayfly pattern

Daddy Long Legs

Wet Flies and Nymphs

Pheasant Tail Nymph

Claret Buzzer

Diawl Bach

Gold Ribbed Hare's Ear

Shrimp   Beaded Shrimp   Beetle   Bloodworm pattern

Teal Blue & Silver   Booby Nymph   Floating Fry

the rising adults. He was to prove that "bulging" trout, as he called them, could be caught, even though they were not surface feeding, by imitating the nymph stage, fished with wet fly patterns but still cast upstream. Along with many other innovations, he realised the importance of timing the strike when detecting a taking fish, and as a keen fly tier, he developed new patterns to support his techniques.

Controversy between the dry fly purists and those who begrudgingly recognised the effectiveness of upstream nymph fishing rumbled on within angling circles long after Halford's death. Many believed the practice was unsporting and that it put undue pressure on the fisheries, and many rivers banned it. "Dry fly only" became the rule on a number of the great beats on the Test and Itchen, but nymphing was to become a valid, effective technique that was to influence all latterday fly-fishing and Skues is now remembered as perhaps the greatest and most influential angler of all time.

In its simplest form the object of dry fly fishing is to imitate a newly-hatched fly resting on the surface as its wings dry, or one that has just laid its eggs and lies spent on the surface. Dry flies can also represent one of the many terrestrial insects that may have blown onto the water from the surrounding fields and bankside vegetation. It's probably one of the simplest methods of catching a trout. Provided the fish is feeding, and you can see it to cast a fly to it, and providing you don't scare it, either with your presence on the bank or because you cast a splashy line over it, you should catch trout quite easily. However it's rarely as simple as that, and there are many factors that distinguish the successful dry fly angler from those who struggle to catch fish.

From the trout's point of view, the river is their domain, and they are masters of their environment. They are territorial, avaricious feeders, sometimes moving around in the river, foraging in the mud and stones for nymphs and snails, and at other times holding station in their lies, waiting for food to drift down on the current towards them. They are inquisitive and cautious, keen to investigate any possible food item but wary of any potential danger. Most will have two favoured lies; one in more open water, somewhere where the current slows and they can stay, sometimes all day, with minimal effort, and the other a bolt hole, a sanctuary where they can hide. They aggressively guard their lies against intrusion by other trout.

The advantage of this to the flyfisher is that if you are cautious, and take the time to observe how the fish are moving and what they are feeding on, you have all the time in the world to prepare before you cast to them

Air and water temperatures play a major part in determining where the fish will lie. In cold weather they stay close to the river bed, but as temperatures increase, nymphs start to rise and hatch, adult winged flies take to the air and this becomes a time of plenty for the brown trout.

To be successful, the fisherman has to first determine exactly which group of insects are attracting the trout, then decide which species they are feeding on, and finally the stage in their metamorphosis which is luring the fish into feeding. If they are taking the nymphs as they slowly float up and hang in the surface film, they will follow them up and sip them in, the rings in the water disclosing their lies. If they are feeding on duns, or spent spinners, look for the tell-tale signs and prepare your tackle accordingly. Provided you don't disturb them, they will still be there when you're ready to cast to them. So stealth, and how you approach the river, are vital.

The Stealth of the Hunter

"A fish's sight is much more highly developed than any other sense, it being questionable whether he has any hearing, or whether his power of smell with surface food is sufficient to guide him in discriminating between a natural and artificial fly. Hence keeping out of sight is a most essential point of study; in fact as before said, the fish should be hooked before he has any suspicion of being fished for."

F M Halford, Dry Fly Fishing in Theory and Practice, 1889

When you approach a river and have taken the time to establish what the trout are feeding on, be it emergers and surface flies or terrestrials, your greatest assets will be your skill as a hunter and your ability to remain concealed. You must be stealthy in all your movements. Trout are extremely sensitive to vibration and will be aware of any heavy footfall. No matter how skilful you are as a caster, no matter how exactly you imitate the hatch, it all comes to nothing if the fish have fled. Keep as far back from the bank as you can, and take your time to assess the stretch of water in front of you. Really… take your time. Try to work out what the fish are feeding on, and how. Always approach the river at the bottom of the beat and gradually move upstream. Remember that trout have a blind spot behind them and take advantage of it. If you are on a high bank, or if there's no tree cover behind you, crouch low, your silhouette against the skyline will alert the fish. As you study the water looking for potential takers, remember that there could be fish tucked away in bolt holes close under your bank. Go down on your knees, crawl if necessary, but move slowly as you work yourself into a position where

you can make your cast. A couple of exploratory casts can be worthwhile, but essentially you are hunting for fish you can see. Dry fly fishing is sight fishing.

If you spot a rise upstream, near to the bank, creep in as close as you can and cast a short line to it. Try to keep as much line off the water as possible. If you can get close enough, although it's difficult, keep your entire leader clear of the water too. It might reward you with an early fish. If you need to wade, do so slowly and quietly, especially as you get into the water. Be stealthy.

When you cast your fly, false cast as little as possible, just enough to dry your fly and calculate your distances. A floating line flashing against the sky will be seen by your fish and will invariably put it down. Aim high above your target, and make sure the fly lands and settles on the water as delicately as possible. A dry fly should float sitting up well, and look every bit a part of the natural environment. A stiffish hackle and an up-eyed hook should help with this.

Trout behave in very different ways depending on the kind of insects they are feeding on, and they will reveal themselves to you through their movements. These are clues that should help you to decide how you should fish

Above: *A fine chalk-stream trout freshly landed*

iron blues have fallen, it's still a great and successful pattern that can be fished both in the early spring and late autumn.

If the fish seem to be over-excited, charging at flies and leaving bow-waves behind them, they could be after sedges twitching and skittering as they try to get airborne. Try to imitate these sudden, jerky movements as accurately as you can, twitching your fly to resemble the naturals. Trout will grab at your fly, fearful of missing out on a potentially tasty morsel.

During the summer evenings when there's a late rise, you will often see trout barely breaking the surface as they quietly suck in spent gnats, female spinners lying, dying on the water. Rises like this are very gentle, the trout seemingly having all the time in the world to drink in these defenceless or dead insects.

If you are fishing one of the wild, crystal clear, stony rivers of the north, look for any obstacles such as fallen trees where concentrations of food build up and where bigger, more cautious trout could be hiding. In the early evenings, if there's a hatch of blue-winged olives, or pale wateries, a small, lightly dressed Orange Quill, one of the best imitations of the blue-winged olive, might tempt

for them and the flies you should choose. Trout feeding on the surface are clearly visible, their mouths snapping at the insects, usually upwinged duns drifting on the current waiting for their wings to dry. You must pick your fly carefully to deceive your fish.

Harry Plunket Greene, a famous Irish baritone and author of the classic book on fly fishing Where the Bright Waters Meet, believed that the Iron Blue Dun, a dark blue ephemerid, was the most important fly to have in your box, tied with or without wings and fished wet or dry. He fished the Bourne, a tributary of the river Test, but believed it to be perfect on all the chalk streams of Southern England, useful "in dark, blowy weather" but excellent on a glassy glide in the sunshine, when trout are refusing everything else even the mayfly duns. Although the numbers of them. Later in the evenings, when the trout start to splash around just before dark, a well-hackled Wickhams could do the trick. A Kite's Imperial is a good fly too. It looks nothing like a blue-winged olive, but you will find that trout go for them when there's a big hatch of olives.

Head and tail rises, clearly visible, will indicate trout feeding just below the surface, often totally pre-occupied with one particular insect, again with all the time in the world as their backs gently porpoise up through the surface, feeding on nymphs and duns and drowned spinners hanging in the surface film.

Having analysed the clues and established what the fish are feeding on, chosen your fly and prepared it with a suitable floatant, you now have to present the fly onto the water and deceive the fish into taking it.

Presentation

As soon as your fly lands it will be subject to the ebbs and flows of the currents in the stream. The longer the cast and the more line you have out on the water, the more the little swirls and eddies will affect the behaviour of your fly. This will cause it to drag across the surface; essentially the line is taken up by the flow of the current and the fly is pulled unnaturally across the water. This invariably leaves a wake on the surface, and trout will almost certainly refuse it. Sometimes it's the line that picks up the current, but sometimes it's the leader, and this can be difficult so spot.

Drag is the bane of the dry flyfisher's life and you must try to avoid it at all costs, but there are certain things you can do to minimise it. Casting accurately two or three feet upstream of your target helps. It means the fly will drift over the fish before the currents have time to effect movement of the fly. Hand retrieve any slack line and keep as much of it off the water as you can. This will help you to keep in touch with your fly. If it drags, ease out a little more line, and let the fly drift well past the fish before you pick it up ready for the next cast, then pick it up smoothly, without ripping it off the surface.

If your target fish is further out in the river, as you cast a long line, just before it lands, twitch the fly back towards you. The effect is to put a snaking line out on the water. This allows the current to take up the slack line before it can drag the fly. You'll find that it'll fish for longer as it drifts down on the current, but you will still need to retrieve line to keep contact with the fly, and be ready to strike when the fish takes it. Strip the slack line in through your fingers, either looping it in your hand, or letting it drop on the water beside you.

You may need to mend the line from time to time to ease your fly onto a more effective drift, or to slow it down. Lift the rod and place the line gently, before the fly gets anywhere near the fish. Short, gentle mends are far better than a big sweep just as your fly is about to drift over your fish.

If you make a bad cast, don't be tempted to immediately pick up the line and cast again. Let it fish out, and when the fly has drifted past the fish, then pick up the line and cast again. It's very tempting to cast straight away, but be patient – otherwise you will scare the fish and miss the opportunity.

It's not always possible or necessary to cast a dry fly upstream. In heavy water, or when you're trying to cast around an obstacle, you may have to cast across the stream, again allowing a little slack in the line. The fly will, for a short time, float down naturally, before it starts to drag, but it may be just long enough

to do the trick. Similarly, you can always try a downstream cast. The fly will drag around on the current almost immediately, and may get some interest from the fish, but not many will take it. It's worth a try if you want to fish inaccessible places, around sunken trees or under the arches of bridges and other difficult places. Very often this is where the bigger fish will be lying.

Fish often feed steadily, rhythmically rising to insects and dropping back into their lies. You should observe this rhythm and try to match it, casting when you believe the trout had digested its last mouthful and is ready for the next. Too early and the trout won't be interested, too late and it will have already taken the next natural that floats by. However, if your timing is right, and your first cast is accurate, you will greatly enhance your chances.

If you are having no luck, but you can see the fish is still feeding, try twitching your fly in the current. If that fails, lift and drop the fly back onto the water a couple of times. Trout are inquisitive creatures – they may imagine a hatch is beginning and could just go for it.

Bigger, older and better-schooled trout can be very wary. They will move more slowly than the smaller fish and be more selective in the food they eat. They will often prefer stillborn and crippled flies and spent females skittering about in the surface film, easy prey, with relatively little effort. They can be hard to catch at the best of times, but in the mayfly season they may be less cautious, unable to resist these fat, appetising creatures. As a last resort, they might just fall for a larger pattern, one that stands out in the crowd, but you'll need to float your fly right over them, without drag, to catch them.

If you can see fish all across the river, and they are taking the dry fly, it's vital that you pick one fish and cast to it, rather than throwing out a fly and hoping one might take it. Rather like shooting at a group of pheasants flying straight overhead – unless you pick on one bird you will miss them all.

You should never give up on a feeding fish. Rest it for while, and then try casting a smaller size of fly to it. Sometimes when a trout bulges at the fly but doesn't take it, it may be that you have the right fly in the right colour, but it's the wrong size – more often than not it's too big. Drop down a size and cast again. Presenting the right size of

fly during a hatch is vital. And if that fails, try a bold terrestrial pattern such as a daddy-long-legs. So long as it's there, and still feeding, there's always a chance.

The Strike

The temptation to strike too soon is something all flyfishers must overcome. Having cast to fish that refuse your fly, having changed tactics, changed your flies, tried everything, when a trout finally takes it, the instinct is to strike. But if you strike too quickly, more often than not you will pull the fly straight out of the fish's mouth.

If you are fishing soft, gently-flowing waters and can see the fish take the fly, wait a beat before you strike, but in faster water strike as soon as you feel activity on the fly. Most trout face into the current most of the time, waiting for food to drift down towards them, and most will turn on the fly and set the hook themselves, so the notion that you need to strike hard is wrong. Simply tighten the line with your free hand and gently lift the rod, and you'll set the hook. Normally you should strike with the rod downstream of the fish, but if the belly of the line is drifting downstream, below you and the

Above: *Drawing the fish over the net*

fish, then strike upstream. The weight of the current on your line will set the hook for you.

Playing and Landing Fish

Once the fish is on, and you're sure it's firmly hooked, keep your rod up and try to keep downstream of your fish. It will invariably try to head for the safety of the weeds or deeper water, but provided you keep the line taut you should be able to keep it away from more serious hazards such as fallen branches and rocks in the river. If you're downstream of the fish, a certain amount of side strain will help you to manoeuvre the fish away from the stronger currents.

Heavier water can put undue strain on your tackle. If the fish leaps unexpectedly, its dead weight in the air could snap your leader. You will need to give it some slack line, and the way to do this is to dip the rod tip down as the fish is jumping. If the fish wants to run, you should let it go, rather than put too much pressure on your leader, and when it stops, you can reel it in again. Some anglers like to play their fish from the reel, while others feel they have more control if they strip line in with their spare hand. If you prefer to strip it in, make sure the line doesn't tangle in the bushes and reeds at your feet, just in case the fish makes another run.

When playing a fish, it's important to decide early on if you are going to kill it or return it to the river. If you intend to release it, playing it until it's completely exhausted is unnecessary and unforgivable. You should play it as quickly and as artfully as possible and the sooner you can bring it in, the more chance it will have to survive. By far the safest way to prevent any lasting damage is to keep it in the water. Never lift it by the tail, never squeeze it, and never drag it out of the water on the end of your line. Try to keep it away from stones and gravel which could damage sensitive skin

tissue which result in infection.

If you have to net it because the bank is too steep or the water too deep, make sure you use a net that's big enough to take the fish comfortably and then remove the hook as quickly as possible while it is in the net. Often, if you simply grip the eye of the fly, the trout will shake itself free. Try not to handle it, but if you have to, then make sure you wet your hands first. If the hook is set deep into its mouth and its removal looks as if it will cause more damage, cut the leader as close to the hook as possible, and leave it. Unfortunately deeply-hooked fish and fish that are bleeding suffer high rates of mortality, but many will survive if they are not too exhausted.

If you must photograph your catch, hold it just out of the water with wet hands for the shortest possible time, but bear in mind that every moment it's out of the water its chances of recovery will decrease. When you are ready to release it, rest it in the palm of your hand, facing upstream with a current of clear oxygenated water flowing through its gills, and wait until it slowly pulls away back into the safety of the deep water and weed beds.

If you decide you want a fish for the pot – and wild brown trout can be delicious when they are cooked properly – then kill it quickly before removing it from the net. A firm tap on the back of the head with a "priest" should be enough, but make sure that it is killed quickly. Then you can remove the

Above: *The upper Cunbrian Esk in high water*

hook, tidy up your fly and settle back to reflect on the great sport you've been lucky to enjoy.

Fishing Upland Rivers

The rushing torrents that drain the uplands of Scotland, Wales, the Lake District and the Pennines provide a fascinating and varied challenge for the angler. The bag may not be large and the fish will rarely be of specimen size, but the beauty of the environment and the satisfaction of outwitting your quarry will more than make up for that.

Upland rivers are usually slightly acidic and do not therefore support the wealth of plant and animal life found in lowland waters. For this reason the trout are generally small, very often running no more than three or four to the pound, though most rivers have a sprinkling of larger fish.

When you approach your river, before you unship your fly and make that first cast, remember that these fish are truly wild and naturally scared of man – and in shallow, clear water they are likely to spot you long before you spot them. River fishing is more about exploring, observing and stalking than about simply casting in hope.

Choice of Rod and Line

For most sizeable spate rivers like the Usk, the Teifi, the Dart, the Lyn, the Ribble and the Teign, a rod which takes a no. 6-7 line is about right. I prefer a longish rod, at least nine feet and perhaps ten for the wider rivers, to give control and to make it easier to lift the line and flies over bankside vegetation.

Small mountain streams are usually narrow and overgrown, so short, light rods are the order of the day – a four or five weight, no longer than about eight feet in length.

Spate Rivers

In contrast to chalk streams, which draw a steady year-round flow from the deep reserves of water in natural underground aquifers, most upland rivers are fed directly by rainwater running off the hills and into their headstreams. This means they may run 'on their bones' for weeks in a dry summer, and then suddenly turn into raging torrents when the rains come. This can be disconcerting and frustrating for the angler, but it can also open the door to rich rewards a little later – if you strike it right.

Ideally, your visit to a hill stream will

not be arranged weeks ahead. You will watch the weather and check local reports before putting your tackle in the car. The best time for river fishing in general is when the river is at a decent height but clear (or nearly so), but you can take fish in any conditions except a full-blown spate, as long as you adapt your approach.

In dry summer conditions, much of the river will be so shallow you can count the gravel. When you walk the banks it may all appear rather hopeless. Not only can you see no fish, you can see that there are no fish – or at least, so it seems. In fact the trout will be there, hiding under boulders or overhung banks, in weedbeds or deep dubs or in the fast water where the turbulence hides them from the eyes of their enemies, from herons to fishermen.

Most inexperienced anglers trying for trout in these conditions make a beeline for the slow, deep holes. These may be well worth fishing, and are likely places for big fish, but if the water is warm it's more likely that most of the fish are in the fast water – and I mean fast. I remember fishing the beautiful River Cère in the French Auvergne in a heatwave. I wasn't really expecting any success in a drought, but I was under pressure to take some trout home for supper, so I persevered.

In the end I got a bag of nice brownies by fishing in water so fast that on each cast the leader was whipped round in a few seconds.

Choosing a Fly

If you have cut your fly-fishing teeth on stockie rainbows, you may be used to catching trout on flies and lures which do not attempt to look like any insect known to science. This approach does not usually work on rivers, because the fish have grown up eating natural food, not pellets, and will turn their noses up at lures which would have a reservoir rainbow on the bank in seconds. They know what food looks like – and it isn't that thing on the end of your leader.

When Trout are Rising

If there is a hatch going on and you can identify the insect, you know where you are. Sometimes this is a simple matter – a hatch of Large Dark Olives or March Browns is relatively easy to recognise and the flies straightforward to imitate. At other times several insects may be hatching off at the same time, and here you will have to look very carefully to see which ones the fish are favouring. You may even find one trout taking iron blues while another is waiting for mayflies.

The good news is that most feeding trout, most of the time, do not have one-track minds but are prepared to look at a range of flies, as long as they are realistic and properly presented. Trout are opportunistic hunters, and they will usually take a natural-looking insect without worrying exactly which genus it belongs to.

Dry or Wet?

Although wet flies and nymphs are perhaps the standard ways of tackling upland river trout, dry-fly fishing is just as effective – and it may even work in coloured water, as I found on the Irfon in mid-Wales once when a friend of mine, an expert with the fly, amazed me by taking some small browns on a dry in conditions where many anglers would have resorted to the worm.

The Upstream Nymph

Presenting a nymph is as delicate a business as the dry fly – arguably more so, as you won't usually see either

Above: *Which pattern will do the trick?*

your fly or the take. Here you are trying to imitate the nymph stage of a fly, where it rises from the river bed to hatch on the surface. Likely patterns include the Olive Nymph and various shrimp patterns.

The upstream nymph is not retrieved as such. Working from downstream and across, cast the fly above the place where you think a trout is lying, allowing time for it sink towards the fish before it reaches it and (as with the dry fly) trying not to let it see your line. The aim is to fish the nymph on a dead drift, so that it appears to the fish to be travelling naturally with the current. If you know exactly where the fish is, you may induce a take by lifting the fly just as it reaches the fish. This is precision fishing and requires care and observation.

Unless you are in a position to see the flash of white as the fish opens its mouth to take your nymph, you will need to use an indirect method of take detection. Grease up part of your leader, and watch it like a hawk. A take will usually be signalled by the leader shooting underwater. How long the leader, how heavy the fly and how much of the leader is greased will depend on the speed and depth of the water.

An effective alternative is to add a buoyant dropper, some distance from the point fly, and watch for it to be pulled under.

Fishing the Water

Much of the time on a spate river, there will be no rise going on as such – just the occasional 'splash' as a fish rises to take some insect or other. In these conditions it will be difficult to find and target a feeding fish. Now is the time to fish the water, which means exploring all the likely little bits of river with your fly until you make contact.

Experience will teach you to recognise almost instinctively where trout are likely to be lying. Until you have gained some, you will need to use your head. Here are a few tips.

- Trout like a steady flow, not a torrent. In a weirpool for example, the fish will not be in the maelstrom under the lasher but in the steadier water a few yards downstream, where the water has sorted itself out and is all flowing more or less in the same direction.

- Flat, calm, sluggish water is generally not productive – you need to fish where there is a decent level of 'action' in the water.

- Trout may resort to very fast water in warm conditions.

- The shallow flats where you can

count the gravel usually hold only fry and parr.

- Trout like to lie close to cover and often hug a shady bank, particularly if it is on the outside of a bend where the current swings into the bank for a few yards.

- Rock formations and boulders in deepish water are great holding places – the fish may lie above or behind the boulder, wherever the current is reasonably steady and they can intercept waterborne food.

- Pool tails are good holding places, usually just above the point where the water gets too fast to fish comfortably.

- Trout like to choose a spot where the current 'funnels' in slightly, concentrating the flow

- On little streams the deepest pockets are likely to hold fish, but on sizeable rivers, trout are more likely to be found in medium-depth water – typically 2-4 feet deep.

Fishing in High Water

When a spell of heavy rain arrives, the water comes hammering down like coffee and the river may become completely unrecognisable. In theory it is possible to catch fish on the fly in these conditions, perhaps by dropping a heavy weighted nymph into any slacks you can find which are out of the way of the main flow, but it will be a long shot. If fish on the bank are important, this is the time you may need to resort to a worm in the slack pockets under the bank. But for sport with the fly, your best bet is to return, if you can, when the level has dropped a little and the colour has started to drain out of the water.

The time when a spate is running off is probably the most productive period on a spate river. On a short stream it may last for a few hours; on a long one, perhaps two or three days. The sport may not last throughout the run-off period (indeed it almost certainly won't), so you need to be ready to take advantage of the action when it comes.

Weighted nymphs such as shrimp patterns and caddis grubs are a good starting point while the river is still high, moving to more conventional nymphs and wet flies as the pressure drops.

Understanding Lakes

Taming the Watery Desert

A big lake can be a daunting place to fish when you're new to the game and don't know your way around. There is so much water that it can be hard to know where to start.

As with so much else in fishing, there is no substitute for local knowledge. Make sure you recce your lake before you decide on a location and a method, driving or walking round it to get the lie of the land. Points and promontories give you a chance to cover more and deeper water, although weedy bays are often the best fish-holding places unless the fish have been driven out into deeper water by angling activity.

In contrast to a river, the open landscape of a lake provides the opportunity to watch what other anglers are doing – and if there are many of them, to see who's catching fish and how they are doing it. If you find a friendly fellow-fisherman who seems to know what he's doing and is prepared to share his tactics with you, hang around with him for a while and learn.

It helps to go armed with a general appreciation of how lakes work. There are vast regions within many big, deep lakes where the trout hardly go, and if you know where they are likely to be, it will narrow down the possibilities considerably.

The Effect of Temperature

Remember that trout need water of a comfortable temperature, which usually means between about 7-17 degrees Celsius. Colder than this they may be sluggish and feed little – and more to the point, their main food creatures are inactive. Much warmer than this and trout, particularly brown trout, begin to feel distressed. So you should be aware of the temperature, to the extent of carrying a small thermometer with you. If you're fishing in a hot summer and the water is very warm, the trout are likely to seek out deeper, cooler water. If a cool breeze starts to blow, chilling the upper layers, they may head back towards the surface. If on the other hand it's early spring and the water temperature is in single figures, look for the warmest areas – wherever the sun or spring breeze has had a chance to warm the water a little.

The Thermocline

As a lake warms up in summer, the sun and wind heat the water from the top and a steady wind will push the surface water towards the leeward end of the lake, creating a slow vertical rotation which mixes the warming surface layers into the cooler water below. The effect of this is that when the lake is warming in spring, the warmer water may be 'piled up' on the leeward shore, while at the windward side colder water is welling up from the deeps. In these conditions, the leeward side will be the place to fish, even if it means casting a short line against the wind.

In big, deep lakes, however, the deep water may remain out of reach of these warming effects all year round, creating a static deep layer known as the hypolimnion. Not only is the water cold here, but there will be low oxygen and

Above: *Devoke Water in Cumbria, a wild natural lake*

Left: *Taking the water temperature*

Above: *Peter Setterfield with a 5lb brownie from Loch Groggary, South Uist*

little or no light. There is little life in these barren depths and next to nothing for the trout to feed on.

The hypolimnion is divided from the warmer layer above (the epilimnion) by a narrow transitional layer called the thermocline, where the temperature changes rapidly in a short distance. In summer the trout may spend much of their time in the cooler water below it, but much of the year they will live out their lives above it.

So in big, deep lakes the watery deeps out in the middle are probably not worth fishing, even if you could reach them. The richest feeding grounds will be in relatively shallow water, three or four metres deep at the most. You only have to look at the lake to see where these areas are likely to be – most likely where the shores around the lake slope gently, not where towering rock faces rear up from the water.

Particularly promising are any areas where streams flow into the lake. The silt deposited around a stream's course often forms a boggy area which is rich in insect life. The stream may have a beneficial oxygenating effect in summer and a warming effect in winter. Fish may also home in on them towards the end of the season when they are preparing to spawn.

An example I know well is the beautiful Llyn Clywedog, high in the mountains of Mid Wales. This is a big, deep lake, and like most mountain lakes it can seem impossibly dour at times. I have had my share of blanks here, but I remember two fabulous occasions when it came right. Both times I was fishing shallow, weedy inlets on the northern and eastern shores and on both occasions I was able to take a bag limit of trout on small nymphs in not much more than an hour.

Another series of lakes I have fished many times is the Elan Valley reservoirs in mid-Wales, beautiful waters which

can be hard work for the angler. One can fish all day without any sign that there are fish in the lake, and then suddenly a rise begins and the rod is bending to a hard-fighting wild trout. In fine summer weather, early and late is the best bet. In such poor waters there is little for the trout to feed on until there is a hatch of fly or a fall of terrestrial insects.

Trout will come right into the margins when they feel safe to do so, which is usually early in the morning and late at night. But here they will be on maximum alert for the slightest danger, and if they detect a clumsily-planted wader or a bungled cast, they will vanish. I have taken nymph-feeding fish in less than a foot of water on a summer's dawn by keeping away from the water and casting delicately from well up the bank. Only when the fish have clearly deserted the shallows should you begin to wade.

Fishing these wild waters is a moving game, and it's best to fish light with one rod and carry all your tackle on your person, moving from place to place in pursuit of fish without having to return to the shore to gather up your kit. You will need a folding net which can be slung over your back or at your waist.

Reservoir Fishing

The rules for reservoirs are not so different from those for lakes, except that they are usually subject to large seasonal fluctuations in level. High early-season reservoirs can be as daunting as big lakes, and the marginal water may be over a bottom of mud or flooded pasture rather than an established lake bed with a rich fauna on which the fish will feed. If it were not for the customary early-season stocking of innocent, hungry rainbows, these reservoirs would be unrewarding places in the early weeks of the season.

While browns, wild or stocked, dominate the fishing in most natural upland lakes, reservoirs tend to be

rainbow trout country. Most rainbows will have been released only recently from a hatchery, where they will have been fed exclusively on manufactured trout pellets. They will still be on page one of their entomology textbooks, particularly in the early season, and are hence easier to fool than grown-on fish. A freshly-stocked rainbow will have a go at almost anything that moves until it learns to hunt for natural food, and discovers that if it grabs small colourful objects whizzing through the water, it will get hurt.

Reservoir fishing tends to get more interesting as the level falls, as it usually does in summer. Many reservoirs still hide the remnants of buildings, walls, ditches and other features, and these often act as an attraction for fish which will use them for shelter or to ambush prey. Many a good reservoir boat-fishing mark is associated with the line of an old ditch or bank.

Choosing Your Spot

When choosing a spot to fish from, you cannot afford to overlook the effects other anglers will have on your sport. In an ideal world we would have the fishery to ourselves, just as every motorist would love to have the roads to himself. The fish would patrol the shallows all day, and we would spot them, stalk them and cast to them at leisure. In the real world, the presence of other anglers changes all that. If you are tackling up at five on a summer's morning and have a couple of hundred yards of virgin bank to yourself, you can fish as you would on a small water, watching for signs of moving fish, stalking them and casting quietly to them. But if you are one of many anglers, and you arrive to find several of your fellows already lined up along the best bits of bank, you need to change your approach.

The obvious thing to do is to fish somewhere else – a less popular, less accessible area perhaps, particularly if you are reasonably young and fit and the fellows who have so inconsiderately staked out your favourite bay are at a more comfortable stage of their lives. Going it alone is an excellent strategy in many cases, but be aware that reservoir rainbows in particular have a habit of congregating in certain areas of a lake, particularly in the early season, and there may be a very good reason why so many of your fellow fishermen have gathered at Rugmoor Point or Savage's Creek. If they are catching fish, your best bet may to be join them, particularly if you hope to learn from them – as you should, when you're new to the game. But if you

do that, bear in mind two things – first, if they are all wading twenty yards out and casting another thirty, there is no point whatsoever in you as a beginner trying to copy them if you can only cast twenty yards. The fish will probably have been driven out of your range by all those lines smacking on to the water.

Do Something Different

There is another strategy open to you. Many reservoir fishermen are remarkably conservative in their approach. For years in the 1970s and 80s, when I cut my teeth on the Bristol reservoirs, the standard recipe was a stick fly (a caddis imitation) on the point and a couple of buzzers on droppers; either that or a black lure on a sinking line. Everyone was doing it. Now trout are not very bright, but they do learn to associate artificial flies with pain and discomfort (this is a much bigger problem if some of the fish are returned to learn from their mistakes). After a season or two I found that I could often do well in a heavily-fished area by trying something no one else was doing – putting a dry fly up, for example, or using tiny nymphs, or a floating fly anchored on a sinking line.

Copying Nature

You can also do well by trying to imitate nature – not just with the pattern of your fly, but the retrieve. Many reservoir anglers fish mechanically, casting out and winding the fly back in the same rhythm all day. Not only does this mean repeated casting, tiring for you and unsettling for the fish, but it means your fly, whatever the pattern, has no chance of looking like a natural creature.

To see what I mean, take a moment to explore the shallows, and see if you can spot a caddis (sedge) larva crawling across the bottom. The movement is glacially slow on the human scale – ten times slower than most anglers would, or could, move an artificial. If you could match the pace of your fly to a caddis,

even one with a train to catch, you'd be lucky to fit more than a handful of retrieves into a day. But you will never do it, because even a slack line in a flat calm drags the flies back towards the rod more quickly than a crawling caddis.

You might think that fishing without retrieving would make takes impossible to detect, but trout that do not realise they are being fished for will often move off with the fly in a slow and deliberate manner, pulling your leader and the tip of your line firmly below the surface. Sometimes it feels more like float-fishing than fly-fishing, but I have made some marvellous bags like this. You will need to fish the lightest of flies on a partially-greased leader, and to keep re-greasing it so that the flies take as long as possible to sink.

Greasing the butt of your leader also gives you vital early warning of a take. Or you can use a telltale – a buoyant pattern such as a floating fry imitation or a greased deerhair sedge on the top dropper. You'll be surprised how often a fish has a go at the 'float'. I took a four-pound rainbow once which had engulfed my floating fry pattern. When it was landed I found that it had already swallowed both the buzzers hanging below it.

The Evening Rise

A still summer evening is the time when many of the flies we have been discussing, in particular the buzzers and sedges, emerge from the water. By hatching in vast numbers, all within a short space of time, they ensure that their predators cannot keep pace and that some will survive to breed the next generation. The result can be one of the most thrilling experiences in fishing – the evening rise.

It's nine o'clock on a fine June evening, and you are sitting watching the wavelets lapping the reeds and putting the world to rights with your fellow fishermen. Lines are wound in and rods are propped up against benches, because no one has seen a fish move for hours, let alone had a take.

And then as the sun approaches the horizon, a fish boils comfortably fifty yards out. Then another copies it, and then another.

Before long the rises are so numerous you don't know where to look, let alone where to cast. Like an attacking army, the waiting anglers all seize their rods, strip off line and march into the water. Out you wade with them, casting furiously to try to cover the rises near your position. But you quickly realise that by the time you have made a couple of false casts, the fish you were trying to hit has moved on – which way, you have no idea.

As time ticks by you quickly get frustrated, fearing that if you don't manage to get a fish in the next 20 minutes or so your chance will be gone for the day. Your desperation will lead to tangles – and there are few things in fishing more agonising than fiddling around with a tangled leader in the middle of a lake, in near-darkness, with fish rising all around you and a dry net. Sometimes the evening rise continues for an hour or more, but usually by the time it's fully dark the fun is all over.

The first rule is not to try desperately to target individual moving fish. For one

Above: *Into a good fish as the sun goes down*

Above: *Bringing a good rainbow to the net*

or fishing on or in the surface. Again, don't be afraid to be different, to show the fish something they haven't seen too much of lately. If the water is calm and the light is right, you should be able to see a dry fly silhouetted from some distance away, and it is a thrilling sight indeed to see your fly engulfed by a vast boil and feel the line shooting out tight to a taking fish.

Don't strive desperately for distance. If you keep on false casting to get that extra yard, you will almost certainly tangle the leader sooner or later, with exasperating results. You will also make fish very wary of coming close to you. Just keep on dropping the fly a comfortable distance away. As darkness approaches the fish will often come closer and closer, until some of them are rising in shallow water behind you. So wait for the fish to come to your fly.

thing, you can't usually tell which way they are going. For another, however quick you are, the fish will be somewhere else by the time your fly hits the water. And it is unlikely to retrace its steps to take your fly when it is surrounded by hatching naturals.

Far better to tie on a likely pattern, then cast out and leave the fly there, retrieving only fast enough to keep it from sinking. Wait for a fish to come to you.

The sub-surface nymph – most often a buzzer, or perhaps a sedge pattern – is the first line of attack in these situations, but if you feel your flies are being ignored, try using a smaller one or a bigger one,

Boat Fishing

This book can provide only a brief introduction to the fascinating sport of casting a fly for trout from a boat. Many excellent books cover this subject well, but here is a summary of the game for the beginner.

Natural Lakes

On many of the larger lakes, loughs and lochs of the north and west of Britain and Ireland, most of the fishing is done by boat, usually owned and operated by a professional boatman who will be your guide, gillie and companion for the day. These watery deserts have very well-defined productive zones and no-go areas (sometimes literally, if there is a nature reserve) and you would, frankly, be a fool not to put yourself in the hands of a boatman for the day. You can fish most of these lakes from the shore if you really want to, but you are far more likely to find some fish from a boat.

A day on an Irish lough such as Corrib, Conn or Mask, with a good boatman and a rise of mayfly, is one of the most exquisite angling experiences our sport has to offer. Likewise a day on some of the lochs of western Scotland where you have the chance of a tide-bright sea trout or even a salmon. If you are lucky enough to be able to take such a day, ensure you are well equipped with a brace of reliable rods and reels and plenty of nylon and flies, as well as

Above: *The late Bar Woodall about to net a brown trout at Crummock Water*

clothing to match the weather, which can be savage. There is usually plenty of room on the boat for two anglers, in which case you will need to respect each other's 'air space'.

Where you fish and how you present your flies will be in the hands of the gillie. These big lakes are almost invariably fished on the move, the flies continually being recast and retrieved as the boat drifts downwind, or briefly dabbled in or just below the surface. Always, in your search for a taking fish you are covering a new patch of water. Takes, particularly from sea trout, often come the moment the fly hits the water, and they can be savage.

Reservoir Boat Fishing

Most reservoir boat fishing involves hiring a boat for the day and piloting it yourself, though many of the bigger reservoirs can field a guide or instructor who will not only take you to the best areas but give you an all-day fishing lesson. This is a great way to learn, if you want to get on top of the subject quickly and don't mind investing a substantial sum.

If you hire the boat with a friend you can share the management of the boat and labour of rowing, where outboard motors are not supplied, as for example at Blagdon Lake. You can also share the fun. Pottering around a lake on a summer's day looking for rising fish and anchoring up in a leafy bay to eat your picnic to the sights and sounds of nature is a wonderful way of getting away from it all.

As with natural lake fishing, the standard approach to reservoir boat fishing is to drift slowly through an area where you expect to find fish, casting with the wind to a new patch of water three or four times a minute. Again you are looking for fish feeding and cruising near the surface which are on the lookout for any small hatching insect or terrestrial which crosses their path. Usually you retrieve your flies slightly faster than the speed of the boat. If the wind is at all strong this may become an uncomfortable business, hence the use by serious boat anglers of a drogue – a sort of underwater kite – which is towed behind the boat to slow it down. But do not imagine a fresh wind will put the fish down; as long as it is not a cold wind, chances are they will be feeding a couple of feet down. A warm wind may bring fish up when the water below is still cold.

Fishing at anchor

In contrast to big natural lakes, where nearly all the fishing is done on the move, reservoirs are often fished from an anchored boat. If you want to present a team of natural buzzer imitations or try the static dry fly, you can anchor up in shallow water and fish slowly and quietly as you would from the bank. This is particularly effective if you have reason to believe that there is a concentration of fish in a particular area.

The Sunk Fly From a Boat

Another useful approach, particularly on dour summer days, is to get down to the fish in deeper water with a sunk line. This does not have to mean casting out a lure and retrieving it; in fact the possibilities are endless. Here are a few:

- Put up a team of natural nymphs on a slow-sinking or intermediate line, cast well out, and let the leader sink towards the bottom. Sometimes fish will take the flies twenty or thirty feet below the boat.

- Put on a floating pattern such as a booby nymph and let the line sink to the bottom in 10-15 feet of water. The booby will hang a foot or so off the bottom, waving gently in any current – until a hungry trout snaps it up. I confess that I have been known to practise this trick while eating my sandwiches – but make sure you keep hold of the rod, because more than one set of tackle has been lost over the side this way.

- Fish the semi-static dry fly. Choose a fly that will stay afloat for a decent

Above: *Drift fishing on Blagdon*

length of time, grease the whole of the leader except the last few inches (to avoid making the tip too obvious to an approaching fish), then cast downwind and wait for a fish to find it, retrieving the slack line from time to time until the fly drifts close to you and it's time to recast.

All these methods have the advantage of reducing the amount of casting you have to do, which is less disturbing for the fish and more relaxing for the angler.

The Fry Bashers

Many lowland reservoirs which are run mainly as trout fisheries also have stocks of coarse fish, typically roach, perch and bream. Each spring these fish produce vast quantities of fry, and by late summer they are an inch or two long and of great interest to both brown and rainbow trout as a food source.

The result is some of the most exciting fishing a lake can offer. The fry shoal up in weedy bays and shallows, and the trout raid them both singly and in groups. The fry scatter like tiny flying fish in a bid to escape, and the trout may almost beach themselves in their enthusiasm. The peak month for fry-bashing is usually September.

If you think this might be happening on your lake, make sure you go armed with some floating fry patterns. Often the name of the game here is not to fish a living fry imitation and retrieve it like a lure but to copy the dead or stunned fry the trout leave behind. Your fly will therefore be designed to hang in the surface like a small dead fish. Patterns can be tied with a buoyant, waterproof material like Ethafoam or Plastazote and dressed with a glittery material like Mylar and perhaps a long white wing and/or tail. A red or orange throat hackle seems to help.

As when fishing the evening rise, you don't want to work like a one-armed paper-hanger trying to cover moving fish - leaving your fly in the right place is often enough. You can take fish very close in using this method, if there are no other anglers casting around you.

This is one of the few reservoir methods which may allow you to actually watch the fish approach and take the 'fly'. It also tends to sort out the bigger fish; I will never forget watching a huge rainbow take my fry imitation almost under my rod top in two feet of water at Moreton Bay on Chew Valley Lake. I struck with my rod too far back and knew immediately that I had not driven the hook home properly. The fish made for the horizon and jumped once thirty yards out like a marlin, upon which the hook fell out.

Small Waters

Since the 'rainbow revolution' of the 1970s and later, many hundreds of small trout fisheries have sprung up, providing convenient sport to anglers the length and breadth of the country. Most of these are artificial waters created by damming small valleys or by gravel extraction, and many are only a few acres in extent. These fisheries are perfect places for anglers who are looking for comfortable, productive fishing with facilities such as purpose-built car parks, toilets, picnic tables, even mini-tackle shops. The banks will probably have been landscaped to allow easy access, and there is a never-ending supply of the most important ingredient – fish.

If you are the kind of angler who likes to be alone with nature and cast for fish which have never been hooked before, these 'put-and-take' fisheries will not satisfy you – and the price of a day ticket may put you off. But when you are learning, or if you just want to fish in civilised surroundings without having to drive or walk too far, they can be excellent places to practise and develop your skills.

While these fisheries typically stock rainbows around the 2-3lb mark with a sprinkling of bigger specimens, some cater for the big-fish hunter by stocking much larger fish, well into double figures in some cases. These are usually the most challenging – and the most costly - waters.

Stalking Small-Water Trout

Fishing these small, clear pools is a very different game from tackling big lakes. The fishing is done at much closer quarters, sometimes almost under the rod top, and spotting fish plays as important a role, if not a more important one, than it does in rivers. In fact it is more akin to chalk stream fishing than the reservoir game.

You are likely to need a lighter line (AFTM #4 to #6) and finer leader material (4-7lb) than you would use on

Above: *A monster 18lb rainbow*

a big lake, and your presentation is much more critical. You may well be casting for specific fish, and spending a large part of your time stalking and studying them to try to determine what, if anything, they are feeding on. There will usually be a fishery owner or manager in attendance to advise you, and perhaps sell you some of the current killing patterns.

It can be frustrating on occasion when fishing put-and-take waters to find the fishing too easy, particularly if you start early. If the rules say you have to kill all your fish, and you get a bag limit of identical rainbows by ten o'clock, you will not be pleased to face the choice of going home several hours early or forking out for a second ticket. But on other occasions, particular on hot summer days, the fish may be as dour as they can be in a big wild lake, and a high ticket price and dense stocking is no guarantee of fish in the net.

An Introduction to Sea Trout Fishing

Despite their close kinship, the brown trout and the sea trout are very different quarry for the angler. They are also very different in appearance, the sea trout, particularly in its larger sizes, looking superficially more like a salmon than a trout. A mature fresh-run sea trout is a symphony in monochrome, its long, muscular body, brilliant silver flanks and dark grey fins making it look utterly different from the freshwater-dwelling brown trout with its warm browns, reds and yellows.

Sea Trout or Salmon?

While we're on the subject, how do you tell a sea trout from a salmon?

Even experienced anglers sometimes get it wrong. Some years ago an angling writer and film-maker produced a film in which he showed in detail the capture and despatch of a fine sea trout. It was only in a postscript to the sequence, filmed later, that he humbly admitted that the fish featured had been a grilse (a first-year salmon). And he was supposed to know what he was talking about!

Size is an obvious difference - in most rivers the bulk of the sea trout weigh one to three pounds, while grilse usually start at around the 5lb mark. However sea trout in some rivers exceed 10lb in weight - sometimes much more - and I have taken grilse from the River Moy in Ireland weighing less than two pounds.

Left: A 5lb grilse (first-year salmon)

Far Left: A 7lb 12oz sea trout from the Towy

So as a beginner, if you get a decent-sized silver job on the bank, you need to look more closely before announcing to the world what it is you've just caught.

You will soon discover that the general 'jizz' (as birdwatchers call it) of the salmon is subtly distinct from that of the sea trout; it is altogether a sharper, more angular fish. The nose is almost as pointed as a tuna's, particularly obvious from above. On the bank, or in the net, look at the tail and the 'wrist' that connects it to the body. A salmon's tail is forked, and the cartilages supporting it top and bottom (see picture) are rigid enough to allow the fish to be gripped securely at that point in one hand – try that with a sea trout and it will slither through your fingers. The sea trout's tail is more or less square when spread out – in fact slightly convex, in a big fish. Incidentally the forked tail is the only reliable way of telling a salmon parr from a trout parr.

Now look at the eye. The salmon's eye is set directly above the angle of the jaw. In a trout, it is well forward of the angle – in other words, the trout has a bigger mouth in proportion to its size.

Finally, a sea-trout's spots are usually bigger and extend well below the lateral line, just like the brown trout, while the salmon's are little more than black flecks and are confined to the upper half of the fish.

The Sea Trout's Agenda

Anglers have known for centuries that the sea trout and the brown trout have different life histories. Curiously, it took a long time before anyone worked out the significance of this in angling terms. The literature shows that until well into the 20th century, most of the experts believed sea trout could and should be fished just like brown trout, with flies designed to imitate insect food.

That's because everyone used to think that sea trout fed in rivers, just as brown trout did. Most books on the subject written up to the middle of the 20th century recommended the use of various natural imitations to tempt them to take. In fact we now know that most sea trout, at least the mature fish, stop feeding on entering the river, just as salmon do. They lose the urge to eat. As with salmon, what's surprising is that we ever catch them at all.

So the first point to appreciate before you set out to catch a sea trout is that its agenda is quite different from that of its freshwater cousin. It does not make its living from the river. It is a transient summer visitor, passing through only to breed and return safely to the sea. It is not interested in hunting for flies or minnows or any other small life form, however tasty. It simply wants to stay undercover, unobserved and out of trouble.

That means the only way you're going to catch it is by teasing it somehow into grabbing your fly from boredom or irritation. And the only time you're likely to catch it, in a river at summer low, is at night.

Let us briefly look at the sea trout's life cycle. Having hatched on the gravelled redds of the headstreams, our fish spends its early life in the river as a parr, usually for two to four years, before silvering up in preparation for the switch to salt water. It is now a smolt and ready to take advantage of the rich feeding of the ocean, but in doing so it has to run a gauntlet of marine predators, from gannets to seals. These killers take a terrible toll of the fish, but nature compensates for this in sheer numbers; a big hen sea trout will produce several thousand eggs every year.

The smolt will spend anything from a couple of months to over a year at sea before returning. The earliest returners are known as herling or finnock and are typically half a pound to a pound or so in weight; these are not mature fish and are not ready to breed. Those which have spent a full year or more at sea are likely to weigh two to four pounds. Once a fish has returned to breed once, it will do so again every year, getting bigger each time, until old age or death at the hands of a seal, a poacher or an angler catches up with it.

Sea trout start running in March or April in some rivers, but these spring fish tend to be few in number, though large. Most of the fish will enter the river in May, June or July, taking advantage of the highest tides and of high-water conditions. A dry spring is bad news for sea trout, because they will often linger in the estuary for weeks before running, becoming fair game for a host of predators, including netsmen, licensed and otherwise.

Sea trout do not run straight up to their spawning grounds, then wait for autumn. Radio tagging has shown that they may swim many miles up and down the river during the course of the summer before finally completing their journey to the redds. They may run a couple of miles in a night, then stop in a favoured pool for a week or two before moving on, frequently dropping back and sometimes returning almost to the estuary. Some fish will feed in the estuary of one river before swimming round to another and running up it to breed. No one knows just why sea trout appear so indecisive, nor why they may spend so many months in the river before spawning, but eventually, in late summer, they find their way to their destination, which is usually a shallow, gravelly tributary, and the job of passing on their genes is completed. After this, like the salmon, they drift quietly back to sea to feed and rebuild their strength ready for the next season.

Tackling Up for Sea Trout

Modern tackle technology offers an extraordinary range of options in

Above: *Choose your rod carefully.*

rods, reels, lines, lures and everything else. However the demands on your sea-trout tackle will be relatively simple. Bear in mind that this can be a rough game. When you're floundering around a muddy riverbank in the middle of the night trying to get to grips with one of nature's most infuriating fish, fancy tackle won't help you. You really won't care whether the taper of your rod is compound or simple, or the reel is finished in blued steel or anodised aluminium. And your quarry certainly won't.

The Rod

It is often said that if you are used to reservoir fishing for rainbow trout, your #7, #8 or #9 ten-foot reservoir rod will do just fine for sea trout. I would not disagree. There isn't really any such

Right: *Hugh Falkus steeple casting on the River Esk – note that the rod hardly moves back past the vertical.*

thing as a specialist sea-trout rod – except that a butt extension, not normally found on a reservoir rod, is extremely useful when playing big fish.

Distance casting is rarely a requirement, though steeple casting – casting with a high back-cast - often is necessary, to keep your line as high as possible at the back to save it from catching the bankside vegetation. Plodding ashore to unhook a fly caught in thistles is bad enough by day – by night it will quickly drive you to thoughts of suicide.

So don't use too soft a rod, or too short. And if you are not an experienced fly caster, don't tempt fate by fishing in front of a high bank in the dark anyway.

You may, if you wish, spend several hundred pounds on a gleaming tool of astonishing sophistication bearing a revered brand name. It will be a delight to own and a pleasure to fish with – until you tread on it in the dark, or run the tip into a tree while trudging in pitch-blackness towards the next pool…

In practice, any single-handed fly rod of around ten feet which can be relied upon to put out a reasonable line and stop a big fish when it has to will do the job. But make sure it has good, tight joints, or tape them up – in the dark, you won't notice a joint working loose until it is too late.

One Rod or Two?

If you have the use of two suitable rods and reels, it may be useful to make up both and carry them with you, particularly if you are not expecting to walk too far during the night. It is a fiddly business putting up a new line and leader in the dark, and this should save you doing so. The usual practice is to put a floating line on one and a slow sinker or intermediate on the other. You may well end up using the same rod and line all night, but at least you can switch easily if you want to try something different.

Once you know your river, you may feel able to leave the spare rod behind. The most successful sea-trout fisherman

I have ever met, the late Rheidol master Malcolm Edwards, who caught more than 50 double-figure sea trout, carried only two things with him when he fished; a rod and a net. There was room in his pockets for all the flies and spare nylon he needed.

The Reel

The demands on the reel used for sea-trout fishing can be considerable. It needs to hold enough line and backing to take care of the biggest fish (I once had an 11lb sea trout rip off nearly 40 yards of backing on the Towy) and it needs to be strong, simple, reliable and well-designed (later that season I lost another big fish in the same spot because the line got trapped between spool and reel, leading to an instant break as soon as the fish ran – I never used that reel again). Today's large arbour reels are a great boon for the sea-trouter because they offer a rapid retrieve, very useful when a fish runs towards you (and they do). The reel you choose should therefore be considerable bigger than the delicate device used for conventional trouting – around 3¾-4 inches diameter is about right.

Above: *The late Malcolm Edwards fishing the Rheidol*

Lines

Choice of line is all about the speed of current and the depth at which you want your fly to fish (more about that later). If possible you should acquire, to start off with, a minimum of three; a floater, an intermediate or slow sinker, and a medium or fast sinker. You can splice special leaders on to the end of each to control sink rate more precisely. Weight-forward lines will generally prove more useful than the traditional double taper, though the latter will allow more delicate casting in situations where line splash may scare the fish, such as on calm pools. The weight of the line should be chosen primarily to match the size of fly you want to use; a big, bulky lure requires a heavier line to put it out than a small traditional fly.

Flies and lures

The choice of fly for sea-trouting is generally a great deal simpler than for brown trout fishing, as you are not trying to imitate a particular food creature. This is lure fishing, not true fly fishing; you are trying to provoke the fish into taking, like a kitten chasing a ball of wool. You are aiming to reawaken the fish's predatory instincts at a time when it is no longer hungry.

It seems that when sea trout are newly-arrived in the river, within a day or two of leaving salt water, they are most attracted to biggish, brightish flies, like the Medicine and the Sunk Lure. Presumably such lures remind the fish of the prey they had been pursuing in the sea. You may expect to catch fish at this time on lures as much as three inches in length (awkward to cast, but they can be very effective, particularly in high water).

However, as the days go by and the fish's memories of the sea begin to fade, its willingness to attack big lures abates. Now the most effective flies seem to be moderate-sized lures of one and a half to two inches in length. Pale flies may still do well, but the most effective colour, going by the authors' experience and that of many others, is black. For the most part your fish are going to be looking at the fly from below, and against the sky black is by far the most obvious colour.

Many anglers like to add a touch of silver to the fly, and perhaps a splash of red or orange. The truth is, silver can only be silvery when it is illuminated by a point source of light; on a moonless night away from the lights of civilisation, it is as dull as lead. As for colour – fish cannot see colour in full darkness, any more than we can. But again, that splash of red will do no harm.

Once the fish have been in the river a while and their silver sheen begins to fade to pewter, they are likely to turn their noses up at big lures, at least in low water conditions. Small traditional flies, even nymphs, may then provoke a take when all else fails, particularly in the low, warm water of high summer.

Ancillary Tackle

You will need the following:

* A net – one designed for salmon rather than trout, which can be carried slung over the shoulder and deployed easily with one hand to land a fish.

* A small tackle bag – big enough to carry spare spools, fly boxes, spools of nylon etc, but small enough to weigh light on your shoulder after hours of plodding across damp meadows.

* A priest (salmon-sized) for those fish you intend to despatch.

* A fish bass, to carry them home in.

* At least one small torch (AA or AAA sized), to see to your tackle

with, plus a larger one for hunting for lost equipment or finding your way home if you get lost. Never trust your night's fishing to just one torch. The small torch should be worn slung around your neck.

* A hook sharpener, perhaps combined with a mini pair of scissors, preferably attached to zinger.

* Chest waders – for all but the smallest rivers.

* A wading staff and sling for safe wading, particular on a rocky bottom or in fast water.

A Word About Clothing

As night-fishing for sea trout usually involves wading, often deep wading, you will need a short wading

Above: *All ready for a night's fishing*

Left: *Surveying the pool before dusk*

jacket, rather than the longer type designed for conventional trouting. You will also need plenty of comfortable warm clothing – anything up to four or five layers, depending on how cold the night turns, how deep you are wading, how long you are out for and how much you move around. A full-length coat is usually more of a hindrance than a help, but a hooded wading jacket is a boon if you are fishing in rain.

Where to Fish

When it comes to choosing a river, a beat and a pool, there is nothing better than local knowledge, and the best intelligence will always come from other anglers. So spend a little time networking before fishing a new river. Talk to the local tackle dealers and angling clubs. And when you arrive, don't hesitate to ask any other anglers you find. Some will be surly, a few may try to send you off to fish somewhere else, but most will recognise you as a brother of the angle and give you honest information.

When to Fish

On most rivers the sea trout begin to run in April or May and the peak of the season is around July, when the immature school fish (finnock) have joined the bigger early runners and the river's population is at its highest. August is usually a good month too, and you have the great advantage that the nights are getting longer again and you have more hours of darkness in which to fish (in June, particularly in northern Britain, the night is a frustratingly short affair). However by the end of August the fish will be beginning to colour up ready for spawning and there will be few fresh fish joining them.

A settled river and settled conditions are best for sea trout. You may well take fish in the daytime when a spate is running off, but you need to wait until the river has cleared and pretty much stopped falling and the weather is calm and fine before tackling the river at night.

Nights when the barometer is falling and a wind is rising seem to be fruitless more often than not. A gentle, warm

Above: *Sea trout in a secluded pool on the River Cothi*

Left: *'I'll take this pool, you try the next one down'*

drizzle, however, often seems to bring the fish on, sometimes producing wonderful sport, particularly in very warm weather.

Approaching the River

Sea trout are very wary fish, much more so than salmon, partly no doubt because they tend to lie in quieter water where their presence is not concealed by turbulence. During the day they prefer to lie low in deep, quiet pools or hang out in shady places with trees or overhanging banks to give them added privacy. On smaller, clearer rivers, it is great sport to go hunting for them with polarised glasses when the sun is high in the sky; it works best if the sun is over the opposite bank rather than behind you.

When you find a group of fish by day, do not make the mistake of disturbing them before nightfall. Sea trout lying in a quiet pool at summer low are almost impossible to catch in the day. You may test them

with a worm or a small fly if you like, out of curiosity, but you will probably achieve nothing except to spook them and reduce the chances that they will stay around to take your fly later on, when it gets dark.

Finding your fish, thrilling as it is, is just the start of the game when planning a night fishing campaign. Sea trout, like pheasants, are moving targets. Just because there were a dozen fish under the old oak tree at four o'clock this afternoon does not mean you will catch them by fishing there tonight. The fish may well be transient visitors, ready to up sticks and head for pastures new as soon as the sun has set.

Graeme Harris and Moc Morgan in their excellent book Successful Sea Trout Angling offered a fourfold classification for sea trout in a pool. The first group are travellers, fish which are just passing through the pool, maybe pausing for a while en route to a destination upstream. Resters are those which are staying put until the following night. Stayers are those which

remain until a change in conditions (usually a spate) send them on their way again, and stoppers are fish which are already near the redds and will not move again until the time to spawn is near.

Now here's the key point – these fish offer vastly different opportunities to the angler. There is every chance that a traveller will take your fly after dark, if you present an appropriate pattern in the right way at the right time. You have a sporting chance with a rester as well, if it decides to move while you are there; this is much more likely if there is a flush of fresh water following rain. Stayers will be harder to tempt, while your chances of getting a stopper to take your fly are slender indeed. If you are fishing a pool for a time and notice that the same fish keeps jumping vertically in the same spot, move on. That fish is a stayer or a stopper – it's going nowhere, and almost certainly not on to your hook.

The key question at this point is – what will your fish do when night falls? There

are several possibilities. A sea trout which has only recently entered the river and has some way to go to its spawning ground may well be on the move again as soon as it gets dark. It may travel upriver for a mile or two before settling in a new pool that takes its fancy, perhaps because it is lined with overhanging trees or is particularly deep. It may then continue to travel upstream, or return to the lower reaches again. Having found a 'safe house' it may stay there for a couple of nights – or a couple of months.

Once you've managed to find some fish, explore further. Work out how you're going to fish the pool. Where are you going to enter, and where are you going to climb out again? Mark the spot if necessary. To quote Hugh Falkus, 'Time spent in reconnaissance is seldom wasted'.

Remember that fish lying in the depths of a pool are probably not takers – they are much more likely to be stayers and stoppers. So don't waste too much time plumbing the depths. Focus on the shallower head of the pool, and particularly, the tail. The tail of a good pool is the number one taking place for sea trout in most conditions. If there are fish hovering here, in the steady glide between the slow depths of the pool and the faster broken water downstream, you have a very good chance of catching them – if you don't spook them first. If the pool has a long steady glide running out of it or into it, even better. You could get a fish anywhere along such a glide after dark.

At last the sun is sinking below the western horizon and it is time to shoulder your bag and your net, pick up your rod and make your way quietly down to your chosen pool. Let's hope you have it to yourself, but if someone else is there before you, not to worry – chances are they will move on before too long, and if it's a long pool there should be room for two anyway (but do ask first, and never wade in downstream of another angler in the same pool – follow him or her down the pool at a discreet distance).

One thing that will soon become obvious is that dusk is nearly always the time of greatest sea-trout activity. You are never more likely to see and hear fish jumping and splashing than in the half hour or so after sunset. If a good fish jumps in front of you as you are tackling up, it will give your confidence a huge fillip.

But don't be tempted to wade in too soon. No harm in flicking a fly out into a fast stretch of broken water while you're limbering up, but you need to wait until full darkness before you start fishing the pool itself.

The floating line is probably the first line of attack for most night fishermen at dusk, but the intermediate may be less likely to scare fish and will reach fish which are lying a little deeper. It will also be slightly less prone to drag, because it gets down below the faster surface water. Is this an advantage? It is almost impossible to say. Personally I prefer the versatility of the intermediate.

The fly to use will depend on the conditions. If the water has recently run off after a spate and is still on the high side (but clear), a sizeable lure is the most likely pattern. If the river has been low for some time and you suspect the fish have been in the river a while, a smaller fly is more likely to work, right down to a size 12 or 14.

Now wade in at the head, as far up as you reasonably can, and start to fish quietly down the length of the pool from the very top. Don't crowd the fish – if you can cover the water from under your own bank, do so. Wading any further out is counter-productive. If there is deepish holding water in mid-river, as on most straightish pools, don't cast across it to fish under the far bank, because that way you will 'line' the fish (put the line across them before they see the fly) and ruin the pool. Fish your fly down the middle first with a short line, then wade down again later with longer casts. Stalk the water, don't flog it. Remember you will never see the fish you spooked!

If it's a corner pool and you are fishing it from the inside (as you should), it will usually have a shallow sandy or gravelly bank on your side and a deep run opposite under a high undercut bank. The fish will probably be in that run or close to it. Unless the river is wide, you may be able to fish the run without wading at all. In that case, you may find it wise to kneel or squat on the sand to reduce the risk of fish seeing you against the sky.

While you are working down the faster parts of the pool, cast at a fairly steep angle downstream, so the fly swings round in an arc below you. Don't bother about leaving it on the dangle, as you might do for salmon - sea trout hardly ever seem to take the 'hung' fly. As soon as it is approaching your side of the river, lift cleanly off and cast again. Where the water slows, cast at a steeper angle.

To Retrieve or Not?

Some anglers like to keep the fly on the move by figure-of-eighting (see chapter on lake fishing) or slowly 'stripping' line back through the fingers, as lure fishermen do for reservoir rainbows. In fact this is usually unnecessary for sea trout, and probably counter-productive in any pool with a good flow. I recommend letting the fly fish round without retrieving until it has fished its way through the likely taking water, then quickly stripping it in ready for the next cast. Slow, steady and fairly deep seems to work best for the bigger sea trout, particularly later in the night.

You may get a take or a quick snatch or two on the first wade down – but just as likely you won't. In that case, unless you have good reason to want to try somewhere else, climb out, walk back to the top of the pool and work your way down again. If you were using a floating line, you might try switching to the intermediate or sinker; if you were using a small fly, you could switch to a bigger one. If you did get a take or a splash near the fly, that's a valuable clue, so concentrate hard when you get to the same spot again. It may be the place where a pod of sea trout are hanging.

When the River Goes Dead…

Some time after full darkness falls, on most rivers, most nights, it all turns deathly quiet. The bats disappear to their roosts, the waterfowl patch up their quarrels, even the otters retire to their holts. No more do you hear the splashes of jumping fish. The graveyard silence is broken only by the sound of your own tired old back creaking as your line swishes fruitlessly through the air. How tempting it is to wind in now and drive back to the warmth and light of home, to a hot snack and a warm bed! And that is exactly what many anglers do.

Yet they may be missing the best sport the night has to offer, and the best chance of a big fish. All the dozen or so sea trout over the 8lb mark I have taken on the fly were caught after 11.30, most of them after midnight.

You see, just because the sea trout are not jumping does not mean they are not there, or that they will not take. Some will be hanging invisibly in the deeper water, while other more restless fish – the ones that are most likely to take - will be cruising silently up or down with not so much as a ripple to betray their presence.

Now is the time to put on a sinking line and go 'downstairs' to the fish, which are probably somewhere around midwater or below. This is the stage of the night at which I unship the black lure from the keeper ring of my second rod, prepared with a medium sinking line and a fast-sinking leader.

Now fish quietly down through all the likely water again, always giving greatest attention to the tail. Don't expect lots of takes at this stage of the night – but then, one take may be enough to make your night. I can remember many, many occasions when a sudden mighty wrench at two in the morning has turned an uneventful blank into a night to remember.

The Surface Lure

One of the deadliest ways of tackling sea trout after dark is to use a surface lure, also referred to as a wake lure. The pattern itself is not critical; the key factor is the V-shaped wake it creates on the surface, almost like a swimming water vole, which on occasion seems irresistible to sea trout, particularly big ones. You cast it out and trundle it gently back, using a combination of the current's speed and an appropriate rate of retrieve to create a steady, tantalising wake.

Surface lures tend to be awkward to cast and can all too easily lead to tangles, but the experience of hooking a big sea trout on one is so exciting that if the night is dark and the pool is still, you really should give it a try.

Playing and Landing Sea Trout

When a sizeable sea trout takes a sunk lure, it usually does so very deliberately. Hooking it is not in question, though landing it most certainly is!

If you don't want to spend the rest of the season replaying the tape of that night's fishing in your head while cursing your own incompetence, make sure you stay on the alert for the moment when a big sea trout finally takes your fly. The forefinger of your reel hand should always remain hooked around the line, so you can instantly grip both rod and line on the strike. Your right hand will be firm but relaxed on the butt. Your net must ALWAYS be on your person, particularly if you are fishing alone, ready to be unshipped with one hand when the fish is played out (and not before).

The first rush of a big sea trout can be terrifying, but if you keep your rod up and your line under control and the fish is still on when the run stops, you have a very good chance of landing it – as long as you keep your head. Sea trout do not usually make for snags; they tend simply to dash for the horizon. Once they have done that a couple of times they are likely to be well on the way to exhaustion. The fight with a sea trout, however big, rarely lasts as long as that with a salmon.

Once the fish is on its side, slide the net under it and lift the frame clear of the water. You'll probably make a bit of a commotion dragging yourself and the fish to the bank, but experience has shown that this has surprisingly little effect on the remaining fish. It's not unusual to get another as soon as you wade back in.

Sea trout stocks are not quite as threatened in general as salmon, so on most fisheries it's still considered acceptable to kill one or two fish for the table. But remember that big hen fish are particularly precious – they carry the most eggs, as well as the genes for growing big. So if you're lucky enough to get one, think very hard before knocking it on the head. When you're returning a fish, if you possibly can, unhook it in the net without removing the net from the river.

Acknowledgements

To Keith Linsell for the beautiful illustrations of trout and salmon, and special thanks to those who provided some fine photographs, including Julia Martin, Peter Setterfield, Sir Edward Dashwood of the Abercothi Fishery and Steffan Jones. Thanks to Annabel Claridge for the photographs of artificial flies on pp 49–50. Other photographs are by Chris Newton.

Bibliography

Halford, F.M., *Dry-Fly Fishing in Theory and Practice* (1889)

Plunket Greene, H., *Where the Bright Waters Meet* 1924

Lapsley, P., *River Fly-fishing, the Complete guide* (2003)

Skues, G.E.M., *Minor Tactics of the Chalk Stream* (1910)

Skues, G.E.M., *The way of the Trout with the Fly* (1921)

Plunket Greene, H., *Where the Bright*

Waters Meet 1924

Above: *Fishing by Moonlight*

Brian Clarke and John Goddard, *The Trout and the Fly*

Graeme Harris and Moc Morgan, *Successful Sea Trout Fishing*

Hugh Falkus, *Sea Trout Fishing*

Chris Newton, *The Trout's Tale*, Medlar Press 2013

Pat O'Reilly, *Tactical Fly Fishing for Trout and Sea Trout on River and Stream*

Mike Weaver, *The Pursuit of Wild Trout*

Malcolm Greenhalgh, *Lake, Loch and Reservoir Trout Fishing*

Peter Gathercole and Peter Cockwill, *Trout from Small Stillwaters*

The pictures in this book were provided courtesy of the following:

KEITH LINSELL

ABERCOTHI FISHERY

RICHARD DUPLOCK

CHRIS NEWTON

RAY LIPSCOMBE

JOE WOODALL

HUGH FALKUS ESTATE

SHUTTERSTOCK
WWW.SHUTTERSTOCK.COM

Design and artwork by Scott Giarnese & Pip Finch

Published by G2 Entertainment Limited

Publisher: Jules Gammond

Written by Richard Duplock & Chris Newton